OPEN for Business

Teamwork can make a business successful.

SCHOLASTIC LITERACY PLACE®

Printed in the U.S.A.
ISBN 0-590-49106-7
2 3 4 5 6 7 8 9 10 24 02 01 00 99 98 97 96

BEN&JERRY'S
VERMONT
Jerry Greenfield
Co-Founder
BEN&
JERRY'S
VERMONT'S FINEST • ICE CREAM & FROZEN YOGURT
P.O. Box 240
Waterbury, VT 05676
Tel.: 802/244-6957
Fax: 802/244-5720
Ben Cohen
Co-Founder
BEN&
JERRY'S
VERMONT'S FINEST • ICE CREAM & FROZEN YOGURT
P.O. Box 240
Waterbury, VT 05676
Tel.: 802/244-6957
Fax: 802/244-5720
100
80
60
40
20
0

Visit a Small Business

Teamwork can make a business successful.

Bright Ideas

A good idea often brings people together to form a business.

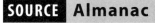

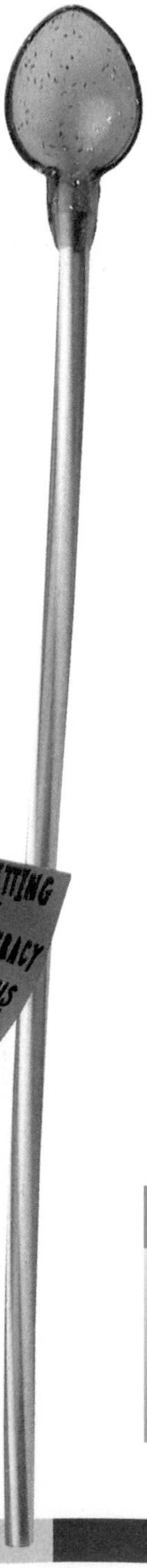

Behind the Scenes

We see how a business operates by looking behind the scenes.

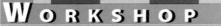

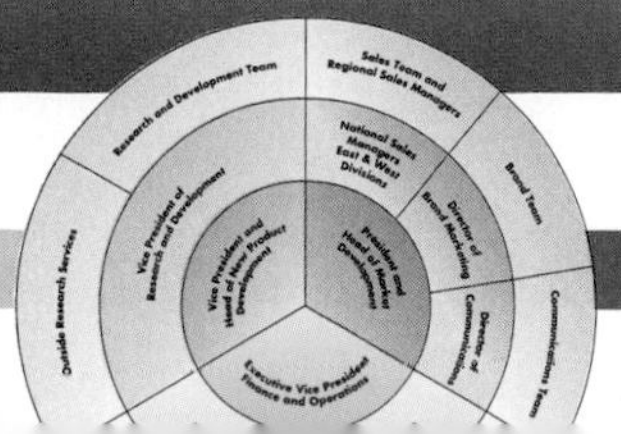

SECTION 3

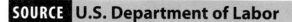

Changing With the Times

Business must adapt to changing conditions.

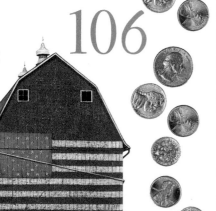

Trade Books

The following books accompany this *Open for Business* SourceBook.

Historical Fiction

Bonanza Girl

by Patricia Beatty

Nonfiction

From Rags to Riches

by Nathan Aaseng

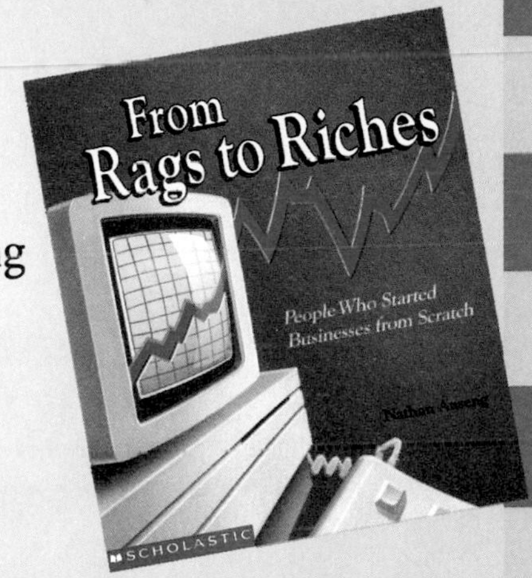

Fiction

The Star Fisher

by Laurence Yep

Fiction

The Turtle Street Trading Co.

by Jill Ross Klevin

1
NEANDERSOLES
OPEN
3

SECTION 1

A good idea often brings people together to form a business.

Bright Ideas

Read a story about one boy's brainstorm for a new business. Learn how you can turn your own idea into a successful business.

Discover how two ordinary guys came up with an idea for an ice-cream company.

Meet the men behind the ice-cream dream—Ben and Jerry.

WORKSHOP 1

Design a feasibility study to find out if your own bright idea for a business will work.

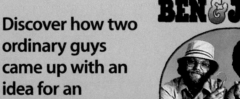

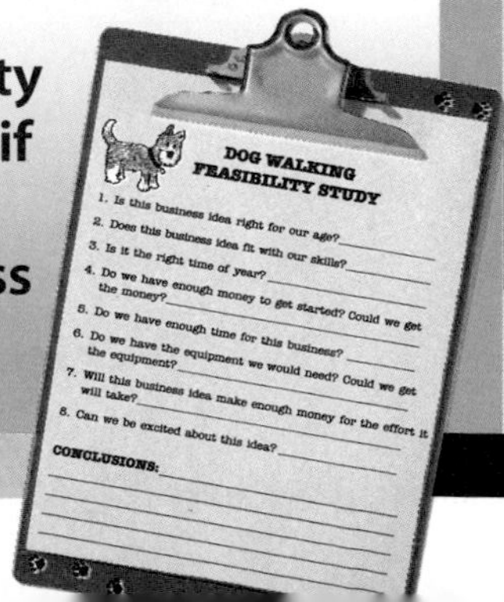

DOG WALKING FEASIBILITY STUDY

1. Is this business idea right for our age?
2. Does this business idea fit with our skills?
3. Is it the right time of year?
4. Do we have enough money to get started? Could we get the money?
5. Do we have enough time for this business?
6. Do we have the equipment we would need? Could we get the equipment?
7. Will this business idea make enough money for the effort it will take?
8. Can we be excited about this idea?

CONCLUSIONS:

SOURCE
The Toothpaste Millionaire
Jean Merrill
Illustrated by Jan Palmer
Novel
Toothpaste
Stock
CERTIFICATE

AWARD WINNING Book

From

The Toothpaste Millionaire

By Jean Merrill

Illustrated by Tony Caldwell

I remember the morning Rufus got the idea for toothpaste. He had to do some shopping for his mother, and I went along with him. We were in the Cut-Rate Drugstore, because toothpaste was one of the things on Rufus's list.

I was looking at some name-brand eye shadow that was on sale, when I heard Rufus say, "79¢! 79¢ for a six-inch tube of toothpaste. That's crazy!"

"It's better than 89¢," I said. I pointed to some 89¢ tubes farther down the shelf.

"That's even crazier," Rufus said. "What can be in those tubes anyway? Just some peppermint flavoring and some paste."

"Maybe the paste is expensive to make," I said.

"Paste!" Rufus said. "You don't need powdered gold to make paste. Paste is made out of everyday ordinary stuff. Didn't you ever make paste?"

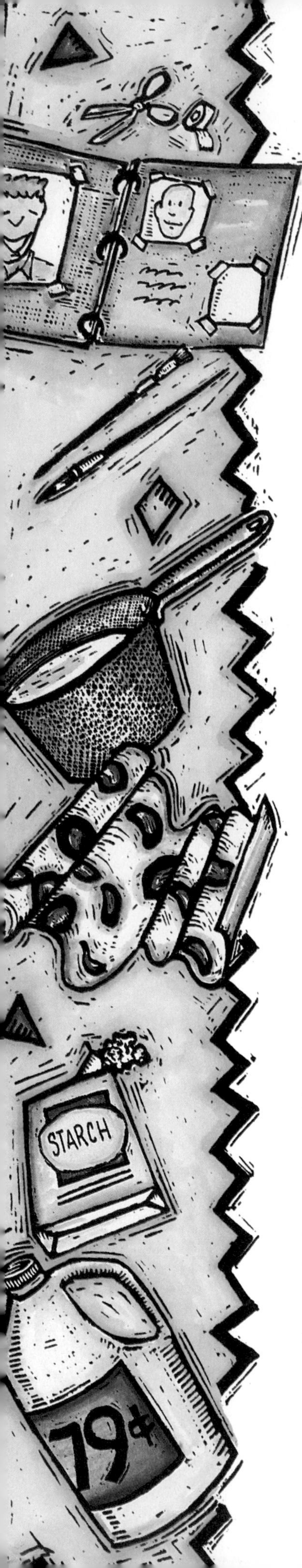

"Toothpaste?" I said.

"I mean just plain paste for pasting things together," Rufus said. "My Grandma Mayflower showed me how to make paste when I was four years old."

"How do you do it?" I asked.

"Simple," Rufus said. "You just take a little flour and starch and cook them with a little water till the mixture has a nice pasty feel. Then you can use it to paste pictures in a scrapbook. Or paste up wallpaper."

"But you couldn't brush your teeth with *that,*" I said.

"Well, I don't know," Rufus said. "I never tried. But I bet toothpaste isn't any harder to make. Anyway, I'm not paying any 79¢ for a tube of toothpaste."

Rufus crossed toothpaste off his mother's shopping list.

"But your mother said to get toothpaste," I said. "You can't help it if it's expensive."

"I'll make her some," Rufus said. "I bet I can make a gallon of it for 79¢."

"Maybe even for 78⅛¢," I said.

Rufus laughed. "Maybe," he said.

"Hey," I said. "Do you think you could make eye shadow, too?"

It suddenly struck me that 69¢ for a smidge of eye shadow about as big as a nickel—and that was the cut-rate sale price—was a little bit expensive, too.

"Eye shadow's a kind of pasty stuff," I told Rufus. "Maybe if you just added coloring to toothpaste..."

"Maybe," Rufus said. "But what's the point? Nobody really needs eye shadow. If anybody's crazy enough to pay 69¢ for something he doesn't *need,* I can't be bothered about him. But everybody needs to brush his teeth. If I could make a good, cheap toothpaste, that would be worth doing."

I decided not to buy any eye shadow. Rufus was right. Who needed it?

In addition to which, I didn't even *like* eye shadow. I had tried it, and I didn't like the feel of it or the bother of putting it on. But some of my friends were buying eye shadow and trying out new shades and talking about which brand was the best, and I just got into the habit of going along with them.

"Rufus," I said, as we rode our bikes home. "I'm going to tell you something I've never told anyone before. I hate eye shadow. I really *hate* it."

"I don't care too much about it one way or the other myself," Rufus said.

"And it just occurred to me," I said, "that if I never buy any eye shadow for the rest of my life, I'll probably save at least $10 a year. If I live till I'm 80, that's $700."

"Great!" Rufus said.

"And if I could save money on toothpaste, too..." I said. "Wow!" I was thinking about how easy it would be to get rich just by not buying things the stores want you to buy.

"How much do you think it would cost us to make our own toothpaste?" I asked Rufus.

"I don't know," Rufus said. "But I just thought of something else. You know what I used to brush my teeth with when I stayed at my Grandma Mayflower's in North Carolina? You know what my Grandma uses to brush her teeth?"

"What?" I asked.

"Bicarbonate of soda," Rufus said. "Just plain old baking soda. You just put a little of the soda powder on your toothbrush."

"*Bicarb*?" I said. "That's the stuff my mother tries to give me when I feel sick to my stomach. Bicarbonate of soda in water. I can't *stand* the taste."

"Really?" Rufus said. "To me bicarb has a nice refreshing taste. Sort of like 7-Up without the lemon-lime flavor."

"But who wants to drink 7-Up without the lemon-lime flavor?" I said. "That's the whole *point* of 7-Up."

"I guess you're right," Rufus said. "I guess that's why more people don't brush their teeth with bicarb."

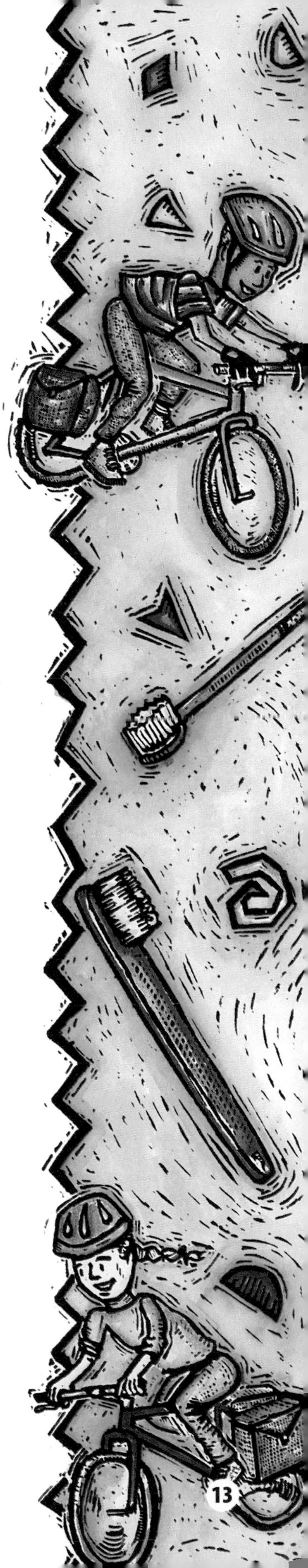

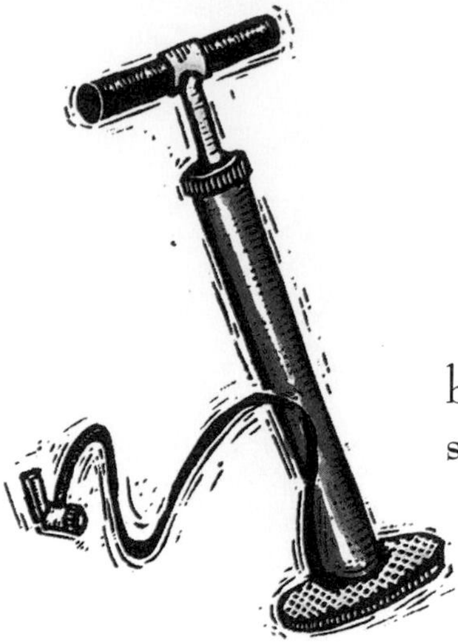

The next afternoon when I stopped by Rufus's house to borrow his bike pump, he had about fifty bowls and pans scattered around the kitchen.

"What are you making?" I asked.

"I already made it," Rufus said.

He handed me a spoon and a bowl with some white stuff in it. I took a spoonful.

"Don't eat it," Rufus said. "Just taste it. Rub a little on your teeth."

I tried a little.

"How does it taste?" Rufus asked.

"Not bad," I said. "Better than the kind my mother buys in the pink-and-white striped tube. How'd you get it to taste so good?"

"A drop of peppermint oil," Rufus said. "But I've got other flavors, too."

He pushed three other pots of paste across the table. The first one had a spicy taste.

"Clove-flavored," Rufus said. "You like it?"

"I don't know," I said. "It's interesting."

"Try this one."

The next sample had a sweet taste. "Vanilla," I guessed.

"Right," Rufus said.

"I like vanilla," I said. "In milkshakes. Or ice cream. But it doesn't seem quite right in toothpaste. Too sweet."

"This one won't be too sweet," Rufus said, handing me another sample.

"*Eeegh,*" I said and ran to the sink to wash out my mouth. What did you put in *that*?"

"Curry powder," Rufus said. "You don't like it? I thought it tasted like a good shrimp curry."

"Maybe it does," I said, "but I don't like curry."

Rufus looked disappointed. "I don't suppose you'd like it almond-flavored, either," he said. "I made some of that, too, but I decided not too many people would take to almond."

"What flavor is in that big plastic pan?" I asked. "You've got enough of that kind to frost twenty-seven cakes."

"That's no-kind yet," Rufus said. "That's just 79¢ worth of the stuff that goes in the paste. I didn't want to flavor it till I figured out the best taste."

"What does it taste like plain?" I asked.

"Well," Rufus said, "mostly you taste the bicarb."

"Bicarb!" I said. "You mean all this stuff I've been tasting has got bicarbonate of soda in it?"

Rufus grinned. "Yeah," he said. "It's probably good for your stomach as well as your teeth."

Know what I did when I got home that night? I mixed up some bicarbonate of soda in water. It wasn't that I was feeling sick. It was just that Rufus gave me this inspiration.

What I did was to add a few drops of vanilla and a little sugar to the bicarb water. And you know what? It tasted something like cream soda. You'd never know you were drinking bicarb.

And I like cream soda even better than 7-Up.

I forgot to mention another nice thing about Rufus. The afternoon Rufus let me sample his first batch of toothpaste, he was trying to figure out how many tubes of toothpaste it would make.

We looked at a medium-sized tube of toothpaste.

"You must have enough for ten tubes in that plastic bowl," I guessed.

"More, I bet," Rufus said.

"Why don't you squeeze the toothpaste in the tube into a measuring cup and then measure the stuff in the bowl," I suggested.

"That would be a waste of toothpaste," Rufus said. "We couldn't get it back in the tube." Rufus hates to waste anything.

"I have a better idea," he said. "I'll pack into a square pan the toothpaste I made. Then I can figure out how many cubic inches of toothpaste we have. And you can figure out how many cubic inches of toothpaste are in the tube."

"But the tube is round, Rufus," I said. "I can't measure cubic inches unless something is cube-shaped."

Rufus thought a minute. "Maybe we can squeeze the tube into a cube shape," he said.

I thought that was brilliant. But then I had another idea.

"Rufus," I said. "It says on the tube that it contains 3.25 ounces of toothpaste. Why couldn't we just weigh your paste and divide by 3.25 to see how many tubes it would make?"

"Hey—we could!" Rufus said. "You are *smart,* Kate. I'm always doing things the hard way."

That's what is really so nice about Rufus. It's not just that he gets great ideas like making toothpaste. But if *you* have a good idea, he says so.

I was pleased that I had thought of a simpler way of measuring the toothpaste, but I told Rufus, "I wish I was smart enough even to *think* of a hard way of doing something."

I *never* would have thought of measuring toothpaste in cubic inches. Partly because I never can remember exactly how to figure cubic inches. And I certainly wouldn't have thought of making a round tube cube-shaped. Would you?

Anyway it turned out Rufus had made about forty tubes of toothpaste for 79¢.

Before I finished breakfast the next morning, there was a knock on the door. It was Rufus. He was very excited.

"Kate!" he said. "Do you know what the population of the United States is?"

"No," I said. I never know things like that.

My father looked up from his paper. "According to the most recent census—over 200,000,000," he said to Rufus. My father always knows things like that.

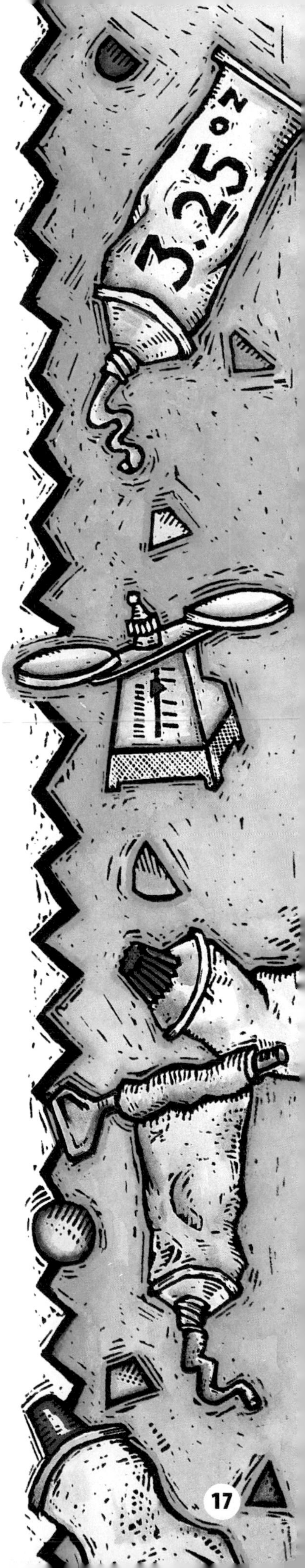

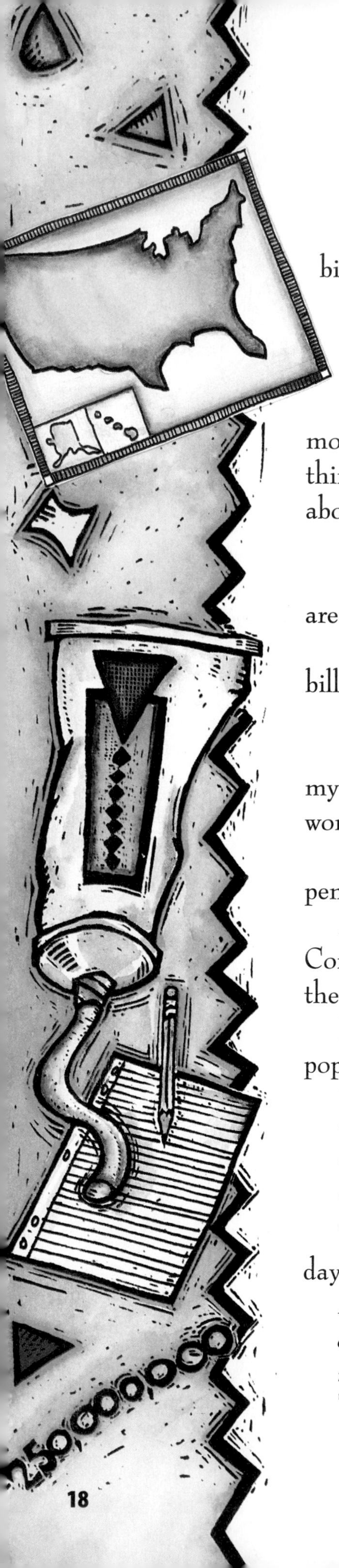

"You're right," Rufus said. "And by now, it must be even bigger."

"Probably," my father said. "The growing population is a very serious matter. Have you thought much about that problem, Rufus?"

"Not yet, Mr. MacKinstrey," Rufus said. "At the moment, I was thinking mainly about toothpaste. I was thinking that everybody in the United States probably uses about one tube of toothpaste a month."

"Probably," my father said.

"And if they do," Rufus said, "how many tubes of toothpaste are sold in a year?"

My father thought for a second. "Roughly two-and-a-half billion tubes."

"Right!" Rufus said.

I hate people who can multiply in their heads. Except that my father and Rufus are two of the people I like best in the world. How do you explain that?

I really don't like math at all, even when I have a paper and pencil and all the time in the world to figure something out.

And at the same time I look forward every day to Mr. Conti's math class. And how do you explain that, since that's the class where I'm always getting in trouble?

For example, the same day my father brought up the population explosion, there's Mr. Conti in math class saying:

"Kate MacKinstrey, would you please bring me that note."

"Well, it isn't exactly a note, Mr. Conti."

"I see," says Mr. Conti. "I suppose it's another math problem."

"It looks like a math problem, Mr. Conti."

The message from Rufus that Mr. Conti got to read that day said:

If there are $2\frac{1}{2}$ billion tubes of toothpaste sold in the U.S. in one year, and 1 out of 10 people switched to a new brand, how many tubes of the new brand would they be buying?

The right answer is 250 million. It took the class a while to figure that out. Some people have trouble remembering how many zeros there are in a billion.

Then there was a second part to the note:

If the inventor of the new toothpaste made a profit of 1¢ a tube on his toothpaste, what would his profit be at the end of the year?

And it turns out that the inventor of this new toothpaste would make a two-and-a-half million dollar profit!

Well, that's how Rufus's toothpaste business started. With Rufus figuring out that if he sold the toothpaste for only a penny more than it cost him to make—it cost him about 2¢ a tube—that he'd soon have millions of customers.

He had to start in a small way, of course. When he started his business, Rufus packed the toothpaste in baby-food jars.

A baby-food jar holds about as much as a big tube, and the jars didn't cost him anything.

People with babies were glad to save jars for Rufus, as nobody had thought of a way of instantly recycling baby-food jars before. When Rufus put a sign on the bulletin board at school saying he could use the jars, kids brought us hundreds of them.

We sterilized and filled the jars. When we had about five hundred jars, Rufus and I stuffed our saddlebags with as many as they would hold and rode our bikes around the neighborhood selling the toothpaste.

We sold quite a few jars. At only 3¢ a jar, most people felt they could afford to give it a try, and most of the customers said it was good toothpaste.

Still, I could not see how Rufus was going to get rich on 3¢ toothpaste unless millions of people knew about it. Then I had this idea about how he could get some free advertising.

Everybody in Cleveland watches a program called "The Joe Smiley Show." On the show, Joe interviews people who have interesting hobbies.

I wrote Joe Smiley a letter telling him I had a friend who had a hobby of making toothpaste and could make about two years' supply for the price of one tube. And Joe Smiley called up Rufus to ask if he would be on the show.

Rufus was very good on the show, though I was afraid that he never would get around to talking about the toothpaste. I was worried because when Joe Smiley asked Rufus how he learned to make toothpaste, Rufus started telling about his Grandmother Mayflower.

He not only told about the scrapbook paste, but about how his Grandma Mayflower had made her own furnace out of two 100-gallon oil barrels. Joe Smiley was so interested in that furnace that it was hard to get him off the subject of Rufus's grandmother.

Rufus told about his grandmother taming raccoons, woodchucks, mice, chipmunks, and catbirds. And, of course, about her brushing her teeth with plain baking soda. But the story I liked best was about his grandmother's name.

It seems Mayflower was his grandmother's *whole* name. She didn't have any last name till she got married. Then she took her husband's name which was Proctor and was known as Mrs. Mayflower Proctor.

But Rufus's grandmother never did like the name Proctor, because it was a slave name. (Rufus explained that back when there were slaves, a black man was sometimes called by the name of the white family who owned him.)

So when Mayflower's husband died, she dropped the Proctor part of her name, and she and her children went back to being Mayflowers. Then Social Security came along and said she had to have a first name and a last name on her Social Security card. But rather than let the government put her down with a slave name, Mrs. Mayflower wrote the Social Security people and signed herself Mrs. May Flower, with a space between the "May" and the "Flower."

I love that story. In fact, I'm seriously thinking about

changing my name to Mac Kinstrey, as I don't care too much for Kathryn. Mac sounds like a boy's name, and boys' names usually sound a lot more forceful than girls' names to me.

But I'm getting off the subject of toothpaste, just as Rufus did on "The Joe Smiley Show." You wouldn't think all that stuff about Rufus's grandmother would sell toothpaste. But then, as my father pointed out, you wouldn't think Rufus's way of advertising the toothpaste would sell toothpaste, either.

Joe Smiley is the kind of guy who is always saying things are the "greatest" thing he ever heard of. Or the most "fantastic." If a girl comes on his show in a pink coat that Joe thinks is attractive, he'll say, "That's the most fantastic coat!" There's nothing that special about the coat. He just means it's nice.

What I mean is, he exaggerates. And everybody Joe has on his show is one of the greatest people he ever met or has done the most fantastic thing.

So when Joe does get to Rufus's toothpaste, he naturally gives it this big build-up. Which is what I was counting on. And what does Rufus do?

The conversation went something like this:

JOE: Now, Rufus, this fantastic toothpaste you make—I suppose it has a special, secret formula.

RUFUS: No. It's made out of stuff anybody can buy for a few cents and mix up at home in a few minutes.

JOE: Fantastic! And, of course, it's much better than the kind you buy at the store.

RUFUS: I don't know about that. But it tastes pretty good. And for about 2¢ you can make as much as you get in a 79¢ tube.

JOE: Fantastic! And where can people get some of this great toothpaste?

RUFUS: If they live in East Cleveland, I'll deliver it to them on my bike. Three ounces costs 3¢—it costs me 2¢ to make and I make 1¢ profit. If anyone outside East Cleveland wants some, I'll have to charge 3¢ plus postage.

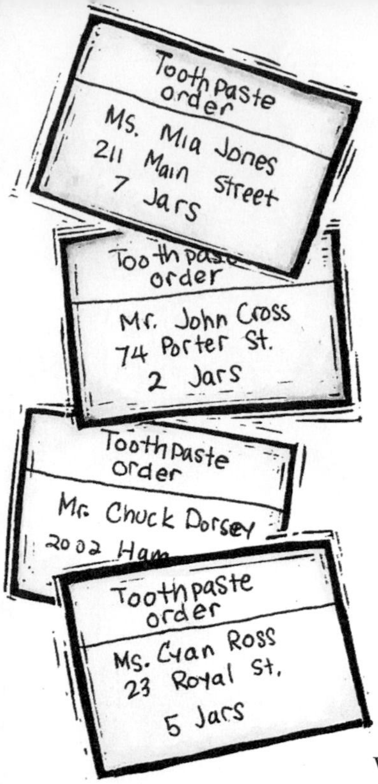

JOE: Fantastic! And what do you call this marvelous new product?

RUFUS: TOOTHPASTE.

JOE: Just toothpaste? It doesn't have a name like SPARKLE or SHINE or SENSATION or WHITE LIGHTNING or PERSONALITY PLUS?

RUFUS: No, it's just plain TOOTHPASTE. It doesn't do anything sensational such as improve your smile or your personality. It just keeps your teeth clean.

Who would have thought that telling people toothpaste wouldn't do one thing for their personality would sell toothpaste?

But three days after Rufus was on "The Joe Smiley Show," he got 689 orders for TOOTHPASTE. One came all the way from Venice, California, from a man who happened to be telephoning his daughter while she was watching the show in Cleveland. The daughter said, "There's a kid here who's selling toothpaste for 3¢ a jar." And her father ordered three dozen jars.

Fantastic!

There's a song that goes, "I'll get by with a little help from my friends...." Rufus couldn't have filled all the orders that poured in after "The Joe Smiley Show" without some help from his friends.

Luckily, after the show a lot of kids began coming around every night after school to see how Rufus was doing. Rufus said they could hang around, but they'd have to help us pack toothpaste.

We were working in our laundry room now. When Rufus's mother decided she couldn't have her kitchen turned into a full-time toothpaste factory, I asked my mother if we could use the workshop at the end of our laundry room.

My brother James had been using the workshop for his model cars, and my mother was glad for an excuse to make James move his workshop into the attic. James is not very neat.

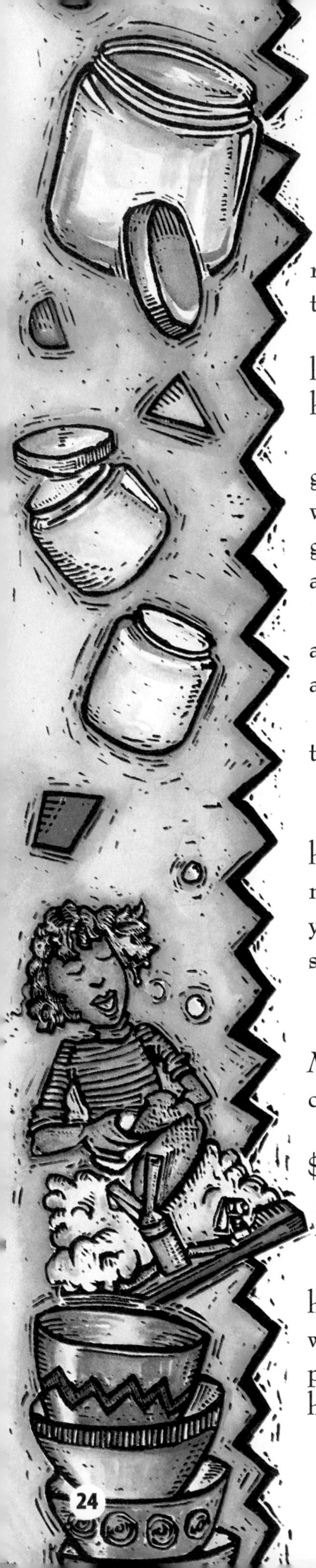

My father helped us build two long tables for the laundry room, and once Rufus and I got all the jars and supplies set up, the place really did look like a factory.

Some afternoons we had six or eight kids on the production line. Some of the kids were from school, and some lived on my block, like Josie and Clem, the two girls from next door.

Josie and Clem were at my house almost every night now. I guess they decided that if I was a friend of Rufus, I was okay. I was glad they were coming over so often, as Rufus and I were getting a little tired of washing so many jars. I never was crazy about washing dishes.

"Hey, Rufus," Josie said one night when she and I had washed about 200 jars. "What would you do if you had to pay us to wash all of these jars for you?"

"How about that, Rufus?" Clem said. "You couldn't sell that toothpaste for 3¢ if you had to pay us what we're worth."

Rufus thought about that.

"Well, I sure don't have enough profits to pay anybody yet," he said. "And I've got to use my first profits to buy more stuff to make more toothpaste. But I'll tell you what I will do. I'll give you all some stock in my company. At the end of the year, every stockholder will get a share of the year's profits."

Clem thought Rufus was kidding. But he was serious.

Rufus had this game called *Stock Market.* It's something like *Monopoly.* With every *Stock Market* game, you get these stock certificates that you can trade with other players.

In Rufus's game there were 1000 shares of stock worth $100 a share. The certificates came in 1, 10, 50, and 100 shares. Rufus brought the stock certificates over to my house the next day to show us.

"Here's how it will work," he said. "Anybody that puts in a hundred hours helping me make toothpaste gets a share of stock worth $100 which will entitle him to a share of the company profits. How much profit depends on how many shares of stock he owns.

Rufus had made up a chart with the names of all of his friends who had helped so far. He put down the number of hours they had already worked.

"Kate's already worked over two hundred hours," Rufus said. "So she gets to be the first stockholder."

Rufus wrote my name on two $100 stock certificates. "With those two shares of stock, Kate should get $5000 if the company's profits work out the way I plan."

"Five thousand dollars!" I said. "Are you sure that's right, Rufus?"

Rufus laughed. "We'll let Mr. Conti check it out tomorrow."

And we did:

"Kate MacKinstrey, would you, please, bring that note to me?"

"Well, it's not exactly a note, Mr. Conti."

Etc.;

You get the picture.

Mr. Conti's class figured out that if Rufus was right about the two-and-a-half-million dollar profit he figured he could make, every owner of one share of stock would make $2500. An owner of 10 shares would make $25,000. And so on.

It sounded so good that everybody in our math class wanted to sign up to work for shares. Even Mr. Conti told Rufus he'd give us a hand if we needed extra help on Saturdays.

"When the money starts rolling in," Rufus said, "we may need some help in adding it up."

Mr. Conti also gave Rufus some advice. He told Rufus that he shouldn't give out more than 499 shares of the stock.

"You have to keep 501 shares yourself to keep control of how you want your company run," Mr. Conti said. "Otherwise the other stockholders could outvote you."

"What did Mr. Conti mean—outvote you?" I asked Rufus later.

"Maybe vote to sell toothpaste for 79¢," Rufus said. "Which would be against my principles."

Naturally, I promised Rufus I would never vote to do that.

SOURCE

Almanac

from Steven Caney's Kids' America

GOING INTO *Business*

CHOOSING A BUSINESS

THE first problem is to choose what kind of business you'll want to go into. Many possible businesses might sound interesting at first, but the only business worth sticking with is the one you continue to enjoy. To start your own business you need to have a product or service you can sell. Make a list of all the things you can, and like to do. If you like animals, you might consider a dog walking, washing, or training service. If you enjoy gardening, you could offer lawn care or houseplant watering services. If you enjoy building or making things, there are several products you could make or sell: bird feeders, pot holders, spice racks, jewelry, and so on. Think of the hobbies you most enjoy. What do you like best about school, or what chores do you usually do around your own home?

To be successful in your business it is not only important to do what you enjoy, but you must also supply a product or service that is in demand—someone must want what you have to offer. Make a second list noting the services or products you believe that your neighbors can use—car washing, baby-sitting, weed pulling, garden hose hangers, pincushions, newspaper fireplace logs. Because you are probably just taking "educated" guesses, it would be helpful, however, if you actually asked your neighbors what they needed. You might begin your survey by asking your parents. Based on your first list of interests, write out several interview questions, and write down the responses during the interview.

ASK THE RIGHT QUESTIONS

Try to be very specific with your questions. Don't just ask "What products do you need?" or "What work could I do to help you out?" Ask questions like "If available, would you buy newspaper logs for your fireplace?" "What would you expect to pay for each log?" "How many logs do you think you might use in a month?" "Do you ever need a helper to do your house and yard work?" "What type of help and skills do you need?" "How often do you need a helper?" "What would you expect to pay for such help?" Ask questions about those things your neighbors don't like to do for themselves, or have difficulty getting.

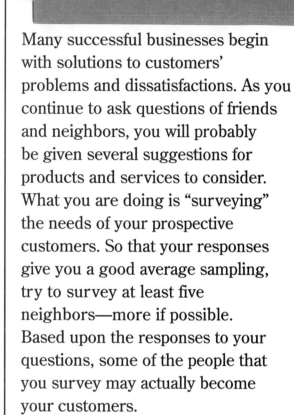

Many successful businesses begin with solutions to customers' problems and dissatisfactions. As you continue to ask questions of friends and neighbors, you will probably be given several suggestions for products and services to consider. What you are doing is "surveying" the needs of your prospective customers. So that your responses give you a good average sampling, try to survey at least five neighbors—more if possible. Based upon the responses to your questions, some of the people that you survey may actually become your customers.

ANALYZE THE RESULTS

Now analyze carefully both lists of information—what *you* like to do and what your neighbors need. How many match-ups can you find? What products or services seem to be most needed that you can and would like to supply also? You may have several match-ups to choose from, or none that seem appealing. You may need to go back and expand both lists with more ideas and interviews.

Before making a final decision—especially if you have several businesses to choose from—there are several things you should ask yourself:

? Is there enough demand for my product or service to keep me as busy as I want to be?

? What is the going rate for services in my neighborhood? Can I earn enough money to reach my goal?

? Can I do the job myself or will I need others to help? Are others willing to help me?

? What money do I need for materials or tools to start the business? Do I have the money, or can I borrow it?

? Do I expect to have competition? How am I different or better than my competition?

The business that you choose is probably not going to be a life-long commitment, but you should consider carefully all the possible choices and base your decision mostly on what you enjoy doing. You should let yourself learn from experience. Your interests might just lead to a business or a profession that you will develop and continue into your adult life—or your experience may show you otherwise.

Once you have made a decision to start a business you should write out a "business plan" describing in detail what you plan to do and how you plan to do it. As you write, try to imagine everything that will happen in your business and what you will do to make it successful.

MAKING A BUSINESS PLAN

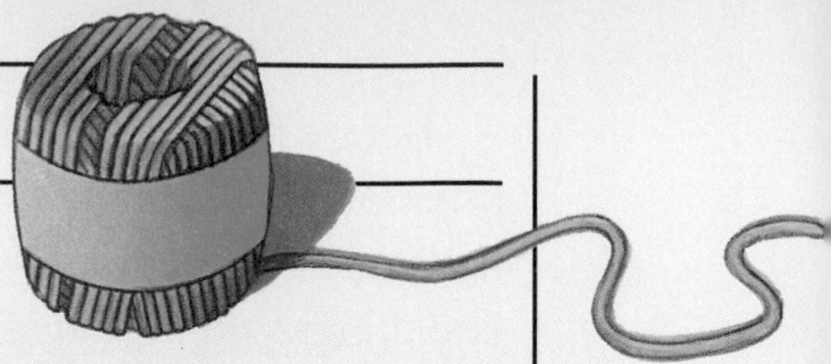

Here is a sample business plan to use as a model.

Give a Description of the Business

I plan to make newspaper logs and sell them to my neighbors to burn in their fireplaces. I want to earn $125 during the months October through March so I can buy a ten-speed bike next spring. I am going to call my business Jennifer's Ecological and Economical Newspaper Log Company.

Note the Need for the Product or Service

My friends in the neighborhood tell me their parents have fireplaces and use them in the winter—mostly on weekends and snowy nights. Four of the nine adults that I surveyed said they burned fireplace logs, and use about fifteen logs during an average winter month.

Competition

Of the four people surveyed who said they burned logs, two buy their fireplace logs at the food market and pay about $1.25 for each log. One neighbor buys real wood logs at a road stand in the country and pays about $3.50 for a bundle of seven or eight logs. One other neighbor has a crank machine for rolling her own newspaper logs. Everyone except the lady who makes her own logs said that they would try using my newspaper logs.

Production

I will collect old newspapers from my own home, and the superintendent of the apartment building on the next block says I can have all the old newspapers that he accumulates and stores in his basement. I will need three pieces of heavy twine to tie up each log. A roll of twine costs $1.97 and is enough to make about one hundred logs. I have saved $5 from my allowance and the cost of the string can come from there. I will use my brother's wagon to collect the newspapers and deliver the logs.

Labor

I, by myself, will do all of the work: collect the newspapers, make the logs, distribute the advertising brochures, and deliver the product. My younger brother, Tim, says he would like to help so I may let him make the logs when business is busy and pay him eight cents for each one he makes. By myself, I can make about six logs in one hour, and I have enough time to make and sell about twenty-four logs each week, October through March.

Place of Business

My mom and dad say they don't want all those newspapers anywhere in the house, but it is OK for me to work and store my materials in the garage as long as I clean up after I am done working.

Sales

There are twenty-two houses on my block, sixteen houses on the block across the street, and eighty-three apartments on the block down the street. Dad says they all have fireplaces, although some people do not use them. I am going to write an advertising leaflet and my mom will make one hundred and fifty copies for me at her office where they have a copy machine. She says it will cost $3 to make the copies and I can use the rest of my savings to cover that expense. I will put an advertising leaflet under the door or in the mail slot of each home. After a day or two I will start going back to each house to show a sample of my fireplace logs and try to get orders. If I need more business, I will print more leaflets and distribute them on two more blocks. I plan to sell my newspaper logs for thirty cents each and collect the money when I deliver the logs.

Jennifer's
Ecological and
Economical
Newspaper
Log Company
Fireplace Logs Only
30¢ Each! Free Delivery!

Sales Projection Chart
Jennifer's Ecological and Economical Newspaper Log Company
Starting Capital $5.00

Expenses	October	November	December	January	February	March
Cost of materials (string)	$1.97	$1.97	$1.97	$1.97	$3.94	—
Cost of labor (brother's help)	—	—	—	2.00	2.00	—
Cost of advertising (leaflets)	3.00	3.00	—	—	—	—
Total Expenses per month	4.97	4.97	1.97	3.97	5.94	—
Income						
Sale of logs	19.80	30.00	30.00	37.50	37.50	19.80
Profit per month (income less expenses)	14.83	25.03	28.03	33.53	31.56	19.80
Cumulative profit	14.83	39.86	67.89	101.42	132.98	152.78

A SALES PROJECTION CHART

After you have written a business plan, there is one more list that you should make to estimate whether your business will be successful or not. By now you know what your expenses will be (string, leaflets, and maybe the cost of your brother helping) and you know how many logs you can produce. From your survey, you can project that you will probably sell all the logs you can make yourself, possibly fewer during the moderate-temperature months of October and March, and possibly more during the colder months of January and February. You will be borrowing money from your parents to start the business and you will need to pay it back from your earned money. If you put all that information into a chart, listing expenses and sales income month by month, you can project approximately how much money you will earn. A "sales projection" chart, as this is called, doesn't guarantee how your business will actually operate. But if you have been thorough and realistic about your business plan, your sales projection will be reasonably accurate.

ADVERTISING

Unless you are able to take sales orders or make agreements for services with enough customers to keep you busy for a while, you will probably need to advertise your product or service to get more customers.

There are several ways to advertise your business, although the best advertising will come from your satisfied customers who recommend your business to their friends. But "word of mouth" advertising can only happen once your business is operating.

Depending on your type of business and your business plan, you might decide to advertise by placing notices or posters in public neighborhood places: the entrances to apartment buildings, at the corner store, on a public information bulletin board at school, the library, or at the local food market. But for most neighborhood businesses it is best to advertise directly, delivering your notice to a specific list of potential customers.

For either type of advertising you will need to write ad copy and design advertising layout. Make your ad brief and to the point (be sure to spell correctly!) describing what you have to offer, what it will cost, and how your customers can reach you. It is also good to praise yourself or your product.

If your advertisement is a poster or a bulletin, it must also be graphically bold to catch the eye of those passing by. Be sure your words are printed large enough to be easily seen at a distance, and use bright colors. A colorful illustration of your product, or a symbol or slogan for your business, are all good "eye-catchers" for your poster. Notice billboards and advertising signs on buses and cabs to help you get the idea for a bold, brief, and to-the-point message.

You can be more detailed in describing your business in an advertising flier to be delivered to the homes of potential customers. Include the same information as on the poster, but try also to state the "problem" or "need" as you perceive it, and how your product or service can solve it. Be confident about yourself and what you can do. Praise the merits of your product. Remember that you are in business because others want your product or service, not because your customers are doing you a favor.

SOURCE

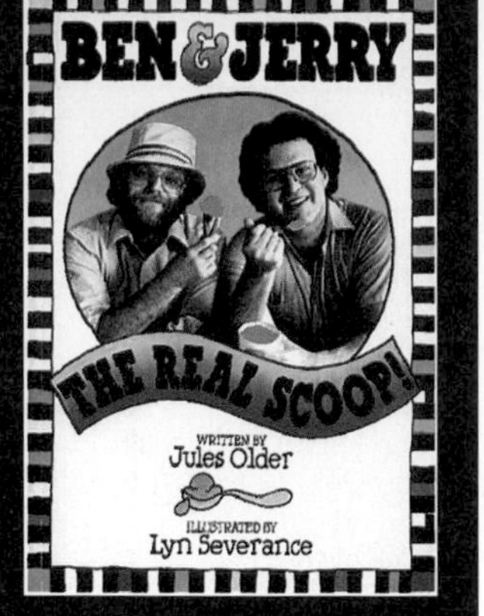

Business
Nonfiction

From BEN & JERRY

By Jules Older

Illustrated by Lyn Severance

How did two American boys from Merrick, Long Island turn a love for ice cream into a successful business? How did they go from two ordinary guys to role models for business leaders all over the world? It all began when they were sitting around one day talking about what they wanted to do. . .

Ben said, "Whaddaya wanna do, Jer?"

"I dunno. Whadda you wanna do, Ben?"

Ben stared at the sky. "The truth is, Jer, I really wanna do three things."

"What's that, Ben?"

"I want to make a little money. I want to do good things for the world. And I want to have fun."

"Amazing!"

"What's so amazing?"

"It's amazing, Ben, because that's exactly what I wanna do, too! Now all we gotta do is figure out how!"

The two pals thought and thought. They thought until their brains were full and their stomachs were empty.

When their tummy rumbles got too loud for them to think any more, they walked across the street and bought themselves ice cream cones.

Jerry bought vanilla fudge. Ben bought strawberry. Then they went back to thinking.

WHAT DO YOU THINK THEY THOUGHT ABOUT?

You guessed it—they thought about ice cream.

They thought about how good that ice cream tasted.

They thought about how much more fun it was to eat ice cream than to mop floors or mash up beef livers.

They thought about how much nicer eating ice cream was than giving—or getting—needles.

They thought about how, if the Fairy Godmother granted them three wishes, the first two would involve ice cream.

Then Ben said, "Yeah, but whaddaya wanna do, Jer?"

And Jerry shouted, "BREAKTHROUGH!"

Ben looked at his pal the way you look at somebody when you've said, "Nice day, isn't it?" and they scream, "EASTER BUNNY!"

"Uh, whaddaya mean, 'Breakthrough,' Jer?"

"I mean . . . I mean . . . Ben, look at me. What are we doing?"

"Sitting here trying to figure out how to make a little money."

"And what else are we doing?"

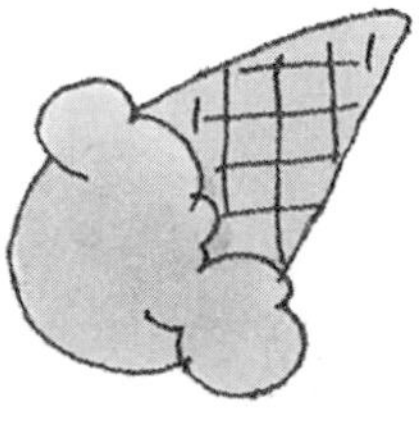

"Eating ice cream."

"Exactly."

"Yeah, but what does—?"

"Don't you see? That's how we'll make money!"

"Eating ice cream? Jerry, nobody will pay us to eat—"

"No, man—we're not just gonna eat ice cream. Man, we're gonna make ice cream! Can you dig it?"

Ben sat and thought. He licked his ice cream cone. The strawberry tasted good. He licked some more. He thought some more.

Slowly, slowly, ever-so-slowly, a little smile crept onto Ben's face.

The smile grew into a grin.

The grin grew into a laugh.

The laugh grew into a great big, ear-to-ear, shoulder-shaking, thigh slapping, nose-snorting, tears-in-your-eyes, choke-on-your-sugar-cone, hee-haw hee-haw, widebelly laugh.

Ben clapped Jerry on the back and yelled,

"I CAN DIG IT!"

But one thing was wrong.

Jerry didn't know diddly about making ice cream.

Ben didn't know squat.

But they knew how to learn. They sent five whole dollars off to Pennsylvania for a course in How to Make Ice Cream. It was something like Carnival Techniques, only eating ice cream was a lot cooler than eating fire.

Then they had to decide where they wanted to make their ice cream.

Ben said, "I like Burlington, Vermont. It's full of students, and not one ice cream shop."

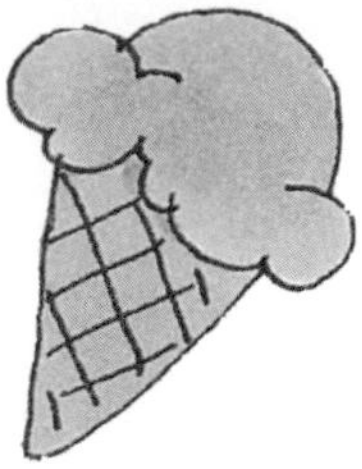

Jerry looked at him funny. "Ben, it's cold in Vermont. Do students eat ice cream when it's snowing?"

Ben smiled. "We do. Let's hope Vermonters will, too."

So they moved to Vermont. They rented a little house on a little island in Lake Champlain. They started making ice cream in a little ice cream maker in their little living room.

Where do you think they got their ice to freeze the cream?

They chopped it out of Lake Champlain. (Jerry was right about Vermont being cold.)

Jerry and Ben invented new flavors. Some of them worked. Like Heath Bar Crunch. Some of them didn't. Like Lemon Peppermint Carob Chip.

Some were great. Like New York Super Fudge Chunk. Some were awful. Like the flavor that tasted like garlic, bounced like a ball and stretched like Plastic Man. Jerry and Ben ate it anyway, but none of their friends would.

As Jerry and Ben tested new flavors, they made a discovery. They discovered that they were getting rounder and more widebellied every day.

You could say they grew with the job.

They knew that if they wanted to weigh less than a couple of sperm whales, they would have to get other people to eat up their ice cream.

So they rented a broken-down gas station.

It had holes in the roof.

And holes in the walls.

And holes in the floor.

And holes in the holes. (It was really broken down.)

They filled the holes and swept out the cobwebs and cleaned the walls, and they were just getting ready to paint a sign for over the door that said JERRY & BEN'S ICE CREAM . . .

when
Ben
said,
"Uh Jer . . ."
"Yes, Ben?"
"Uh, Jer . . ."
he
said
again.
"Yes, Ben?"

Ben took a deep breath. "Uh, Jer, Idon'tthinkJERRY&BEN'Ssoundsasniceas . . . as . . . as . . ."

"Yes, Ben?"

"As, well er um uh as . . . BEN & JERRY'S."

"Yes, Ben."

"You mean it, Jer? BEN & JERRY'S—you can dig it?"

"I can dig it."

"Like wow! We'll call it BEN & JERRY'S. BEN & JERRY'S HOMEMADE. And because your name comes second, you can be President!"

"And because your name comes first, Ben, I hereby anoint you Vice President. Ta Da!"

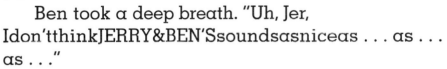

GREAT in ICE CREAM

START HERE

1963 Jerry Greenfield and Ben Cohen meet in seventh grade gym class.

1977 Jerry and Ben move to Vermont and take a $5 course in How to Make Ice Cream.

1978 The guys scoop their first cone on May 5 at the gas station in Burlington, Vermont. (The station is gone, but there's a plaque on the corner of College and St. Paul Streets where it once stood.)

1980 Introducing... Ben & Jerry's in Pints!

1983 Ben & Jerry's builds the world's biggest ice cream sundae on April 15 in St. Albans, Vermont. It weighs 27,102 pounds.

MOMENTS HISTORY...

1986

1987

This is the year Ben & Jerry's opens in Canada and Israel. (The Israeli T-shirts read from right to left.)

A new flavor is born—CHERRY GARCIA! It's their third most popular flavor—Ta da!

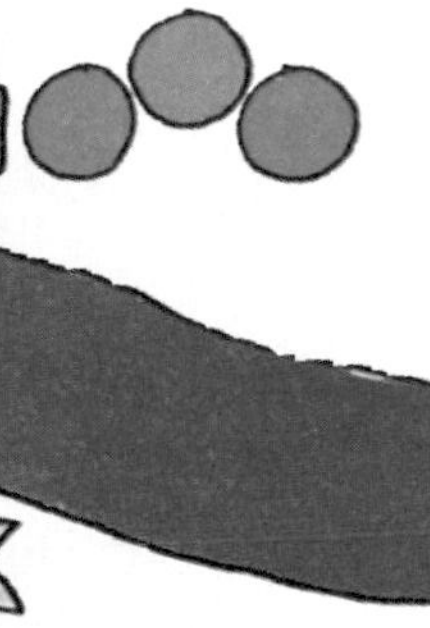

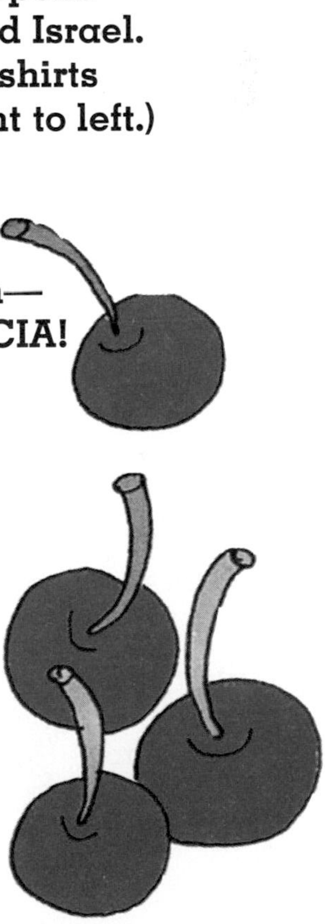

STILL 1986

Ben & Jerry's opens its new ice cream factory in Waterbury, Vermont. They give tours... and free samples, too.

Meanwhile, in Cleveland, Ohio, Cowmobile burns up, creating the world's biggest Baked Alaska.

1988

Ben & Jerry are named Small (sic) Business Persons of the Year by the President of the United States. At the White House ceremony, the guys wear ties. (They've never worn 'em again.)

More than 200,000 people tour the Ben & Jerry's factory.

1989

Introducing... RAINFOREST CRUNCH!

1990

Introducing... FRESH GEORGIA PEACH and WILD MAINE BLUEBERRY.

1991

On the ice cream front, Chocolate Chip Cookie Dough is released in pints and rockets to the top of the Most Popular Flavor in Pints list.

STILL 1991

And the University of Vermont makes Ben & Jerry honorary doctors of law. The crowd gives them a standing ovation.

On the entertainment front, Vermont, Chicago and San Francisco host the first One World, One Heart Festivals.

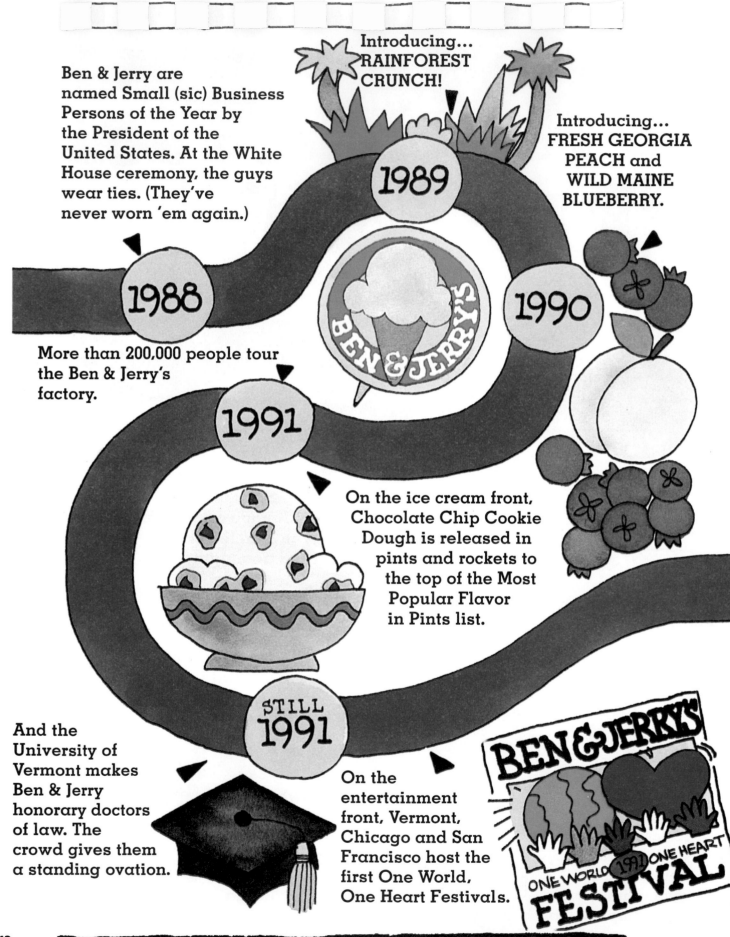

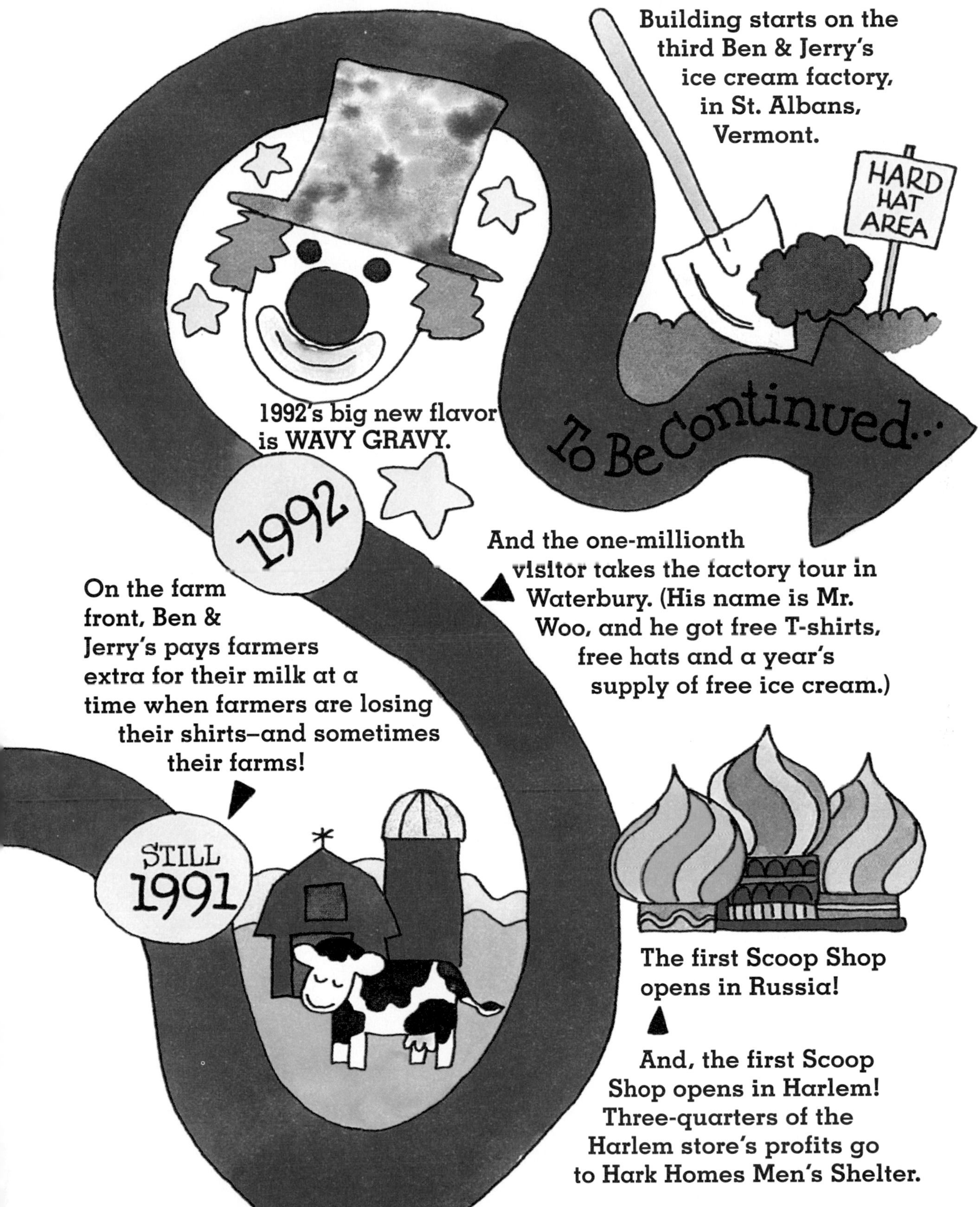

Building starts on the third Ben & Jerry's ice cream factory, in St. Albans, Vermont.

1992's big new flavor is WAVY GRAVY.

And the one-millionth visitor takes the factory tour in Waterbury. (His name is Mr. Woo, and he got free T-shirts, free hats and a year's supply of free ice cream.)

On the farm front, Ben & Jerry's pays farmers extra for their milk at a time when farmers are losing their shirts–and sometimes their farms!

The first Scoop Shop opens in Russia!

And, the first Scoop Shop opens in Harlem! Three-quarters of the Harlem store's profits go to Hark Homes Men's Shelter.

Ben and Jerry

Entrepreneurs

These guys make the office a fun place to be.

Is it possible to take one small idea and turn it into a huge business success? If you ask entrepreneurs Ben Cohen and Jerry Greenfield, they'll say yes. But they'll also tell you that running a successful business is a team effort. Ben and Jerry have over 600 employees on their team. That's a lot of people, but judging by the success of their product, Ben and Jerry's team members must work together very well.

PROFILE

Names:
Ben Cohen
Jerry Greenfield

Occupation:
co-founders of Ben & Jerry's

Favorite flavors:
Ben: Wavy Gravy
Jerry: Chocolate Fudge Brownie frozen yogurt

Former careers:
Ben: truck driver, taxi driver, hamburger flipper, school cook, crafts teacher
Jerry: ice-cream scooper, lab technician, driver

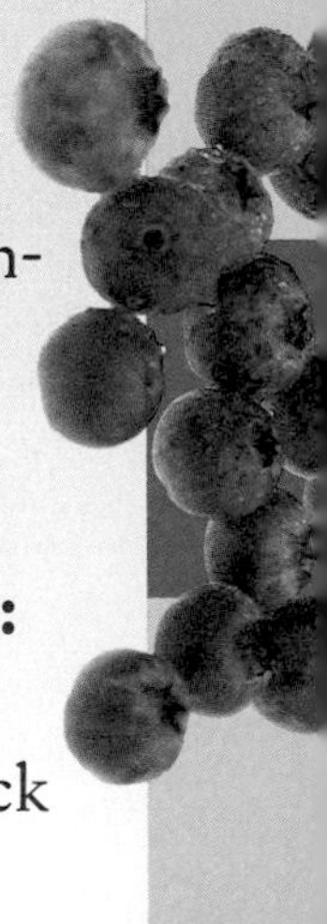

Original duties at Ben & Jerry's:
Ben: scooper, taste-tester, truck driver
Jerry: ice-cream maker

MORE ABOUT
Ben and Jerry

Inside the Plant

It's morning at Ben & Jerry's ice-cream manufacturing plant in Waterbury, Vermont. Workers are deciding which tasks to do for the day. Some will mix ingredients. Others will blend "chunks" into the ice cream. Still others will wrap the ice-cream containers into 8-pint bundles. Since everyone knows each step of the ice-cream-making process, no one has to do the same job every day. Ben and Jerry planned it that way to help keep employees happy and productive.

Fun on the Job

The two bosses have a motto: "If it's no fun, why do it?" How have they incorporated this philosophy in the workplace? Among other things, employees get three free pints of ice cream a day (plus chocolate chip cookies on Fridays), free time at a health club to work off all those extra calories, and free back rubs and foot rubs.

On the practical side, the company sets aside 5 percent of its profits for workers to share. The company also provides on-site day care for

workers' children. And when those children get older, there's a tuition-assistance program to help pay for their college education.

Who's Who?

Although they're often thought of as a team, Ben and Jerry have their own distinct personalities. Company workers think of Ben as the "idea man." At meetings, he's always saying "Here's an idea" or "Let's try this."

If Ben is considered the creative one, Jerry is known as the great communicator. "Jerry may show up at the plant in the middle of the night and walk around talking and helping out the people on the night shift," says company spokesperson Lee Holden. Jerry also communicates with stockholders and the Ben & Jerry's franchises across the country.

Community Concern

Ben and Jerry are serious about helping others. Their ideas about teamwork extend beyond their own employees. Ben and Jerry have set up a Social Mission Department to suggest groups and causes that the company might be interested in.

Ben is proud of the community work the company does. "We've opened an ice-cream plant in Russia after working with our Russian partners," he says. "And in Harlem we've opened a scoop shop whose profits will help the homeless." According to Ben, "It's fun to help make our lives and other people's lives better. After all, if it weren't fun, we probably wouldn't do it!"

Ben and Jerry's Tips for Building an Effective Team

1. Communication is essential. Meetings, newsletters, and bulletin-board notices can help teammates keep in touch.
2. Try to make each team member's job interesting and fun. Teammates may want to learn one another's jobs and take turns doing different tasks.
3. Offering incentives—bringing snacks to team meetings, for example—is a good way to motivate a team.

WORKSHOP 1

How to

Design a Feasibility Study

A feasibility study often begins by listing questions. The goal of the study is to answer these questions.

All businesses start with a good idea. But some ideas are more practical than others. Conducting a feasibility study is one way to find out whether a bright idea will really work.

What is a feasibility study? A feasibility study is a document that helps determine if a business idea is "feasible"—that is, does it have a good chance of succeeding? The study includes a list of questions about a business idea. Researching and analyzing the answers to these questions can help entrepreneurs decide whether to go ahead with the idea.

The title names the business.

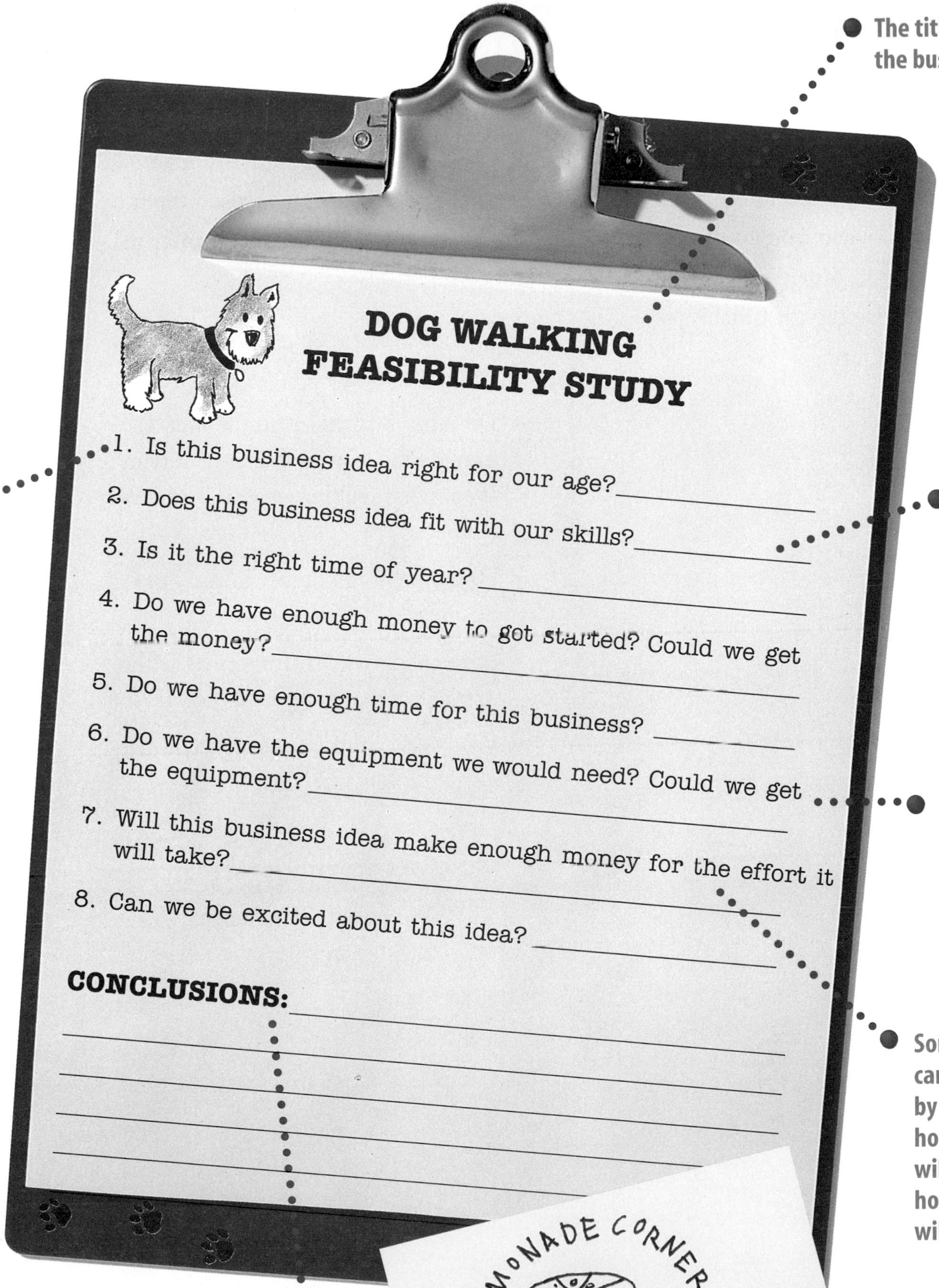

DOG WALKING FEASIBILITY STUDY

1. Is this business idea right for our age?__________
2. Does this business idea fit with our skills?__________
3. Is it the right time of year? __________
4. Do we have enough money to get started? Could we get the money?__________
5. Do we have enough time for this business? __________
6. Do we have the equipment we would need? Could we get the equipment?__________
7. Will this business idea make enough money for the effort it will take?__________
8. Can we be excited about this idea? __________

CONCLUSIONS: __________

Some questions can be answered by listing everyone's skills.

Some questions can be answered by doing research.

Some questions can be answered by estimating how much things will cost, and how much money will be made.

This section will discuss whether or not the idea is feasible.

1 Brainstorm Ideas

Form a group and brainstorm a list of businesses that might be fun to start. Think about products you could sell or services you could provide. Work together to choose the idea that most interests your group.

TOOLS

- notebook and pencil
- markers
- newsprint or posterboard
- local telephone directory
- local newspapers

2 Ask Questions

Design a feasibility study to determine whether your idea can succeed. Start by creating a list of questions, such as the following:

- Is your product or service needed in your community?
- Do other businesses in the area provide the same product or service? If so, what will make your business better?
- How much will it cost to run your business?
- How much will customers be willing to pay for your product or service?
- What skills and knowledge will be needed to operate your business?

Tip Be creative. Try a business idea that no one has ever thought of before—or put a new twist on an old idea.

3 Research

Divide a sheet of chart paper into two columns labeled "Questions" and "Answers." Write your list of questions in the appropriate column.

With your teammates, look for answers to the questions. You can work together or divide up the questions and work independently. Your research might include some of the following tasks:

- talking to friends and neighbors to find out whether they're interested in your product or service
- looking at local newspaper and phone book ads to uncover potential competitors
- visiting competitors to find out what they're offering and how much they charge
- talking with your team to decide how each member can contribute to the business

4 Analyze Your Results

When your research is complete, fill in the "Answers" column on your chart. Analyze the answers you've found. Is there enough demand for your product or service? How much will it cost to provide? Does your team have the necessary skills and information to run your business? Record your conclusions at the bottom of the chart. State whether your idea is feasible, and briefly explain why or why not.

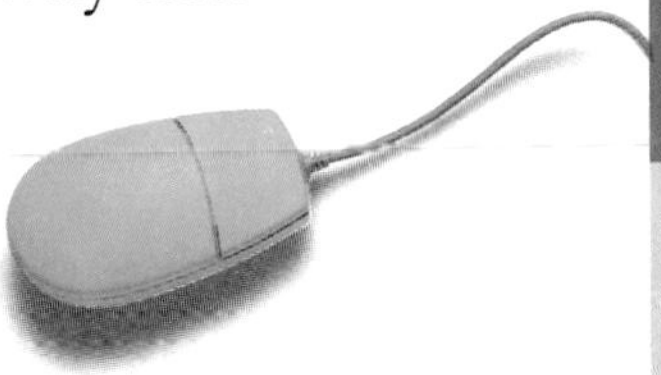

If You Are Using a Computer . . .

Create a survey about your business idea to find out if other people will be interested in your service or product. You can send this survey on-line, and discuss the responses with your teammates.

THINK

What do you think is the most important ingredient of a successful business?

Ben and Jerry
Entrepreneurs

FLOUR
FLOUR

SECTION 2

We see how a business operates by looking behind the scenes.

Behind the Scenes

Find out what it's like to run a business by reading a story about a young entrepreneur. See how a real-life group of city kids run their own company.

Follow a pair of jeans from the time it's just an idea until it hits the store shelves. Meet the man who invented the first pair of jeans.

WORKSHOP 2

Create an organizational chart that will show how people will work together in your business.

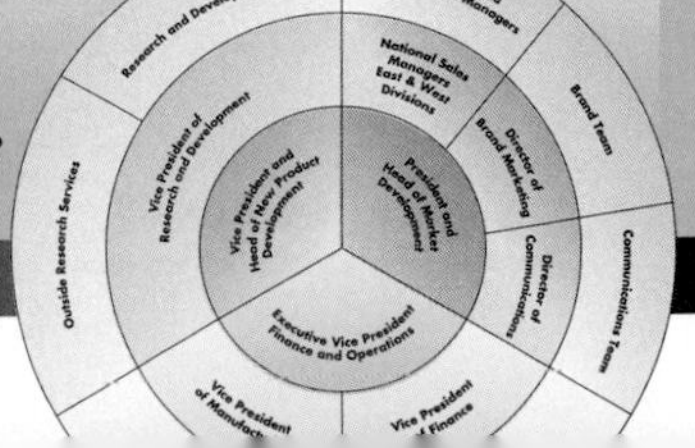

SOURCE

Novel

From

AWARD WINNING Author

EDDIE ANSELMINO WANTED A JOB, BUT NOT JUST ANY JOB. HE AND HIS FRIENDS WERE DETERMINED TO START THEIR OWN BUSINESS. IT WASN'T EASY. THEY KNEW THAT ANY NEW BUSINESS WOULD HAVE TO FILL A NEED OR SOLVE A PROBLEM. BUT WHAT PROBLEM COULD THREE SIXTH-GRADERS SOLVE? NO ONE BELIEVED IN THEM, UNTIL EDDIE CAME UP WITH AN IDEA.

BY PHYLLIS REYNOLDS NAYLOR

ILLUSTRATED BY MIN JAE HONG

AT BREAKFAST the next morning, he made his announcement.

"I've found it!" he said. "I've found a problem!"

"I thought you were looking for a job," said Joseph.

"Find a problem, and you've got yourself a business," Eddie told him. And then he explained his idea.

There were too many kids in South End, that's what. There might be a lot of sixth graders needing protection. But there were a whole lot more little kids. There were more and more tricycles to fall over on the sidewalk and more and more toddlers to hide in Mr. Anselmino's potato bin. Which meant that there were dozens and dozens of parents wanting to get away from it all for an evening or two, and dozens and dozens of babies that needed sitting. But—as the want ads in the *South End Weekly* should have shown him—there weren't that many older children willing to sit them.

That was the problem.

"I'm going to run a sitting service," Eddie told his family. "I'm going to start an agency."

He watched for the faintest sign of a frown or a cough or a smirk, but there weren't any.

"I tell you what you need," said Roger. "A contract. You've got to have a contract. You've got to make it so the parents know what they're getting and the sitters know what to expect."

Mrs. Anselmino nodded. "And you've got to be reliable. You've got to have substitutes so that if one sitter can't make it, you'll have somebody to take his place."

"And decide on your fee," said Mr. Anselmino. "Either a percentage of the payment, or a flat fee."

Joseph was quiet for a moment. "I wish I'd thought of this," he said finally.

But Eddie was one step ahead of them. He was already working it out in his head, and by the time he called Dink and Elizabeth over, he knew just how it was going to be.

"When parents need a sitter," he explained, "they won't have to make seven or eight phone calls before they find one. All they'll have to do is call our agency, and we'll find the sitter for them."

"But hardly any of the kids at school want to sit," said Elizabeth.

"And some of the parents complain about the ones who do," said Dink.

"Exactly," said Eddie. "We've got to find out why and write up two contracts. Both sitters and parents will have to sign a contract before we take them on as clients."

Clients. Eddie loved the word. It slid off his tongue like a butter cream. *Clients. Contracts. Percentages. Profits.*

Eddie, Dink, and Elizabeth spent the first Saturday interviewing parents about what they expected of a sitter. They spent the second Saturday talking with their friends about what they expected on a job. Then they wrote up the two contracts:

I

A Sitter is expected to:

1. Be on time.
2. Avoid long conversations on the phone with friends.
3. Eat only what he has been told he can eat.
4. Give full attention to the child and not spend the evening in front of the TV.
5. Leave the house as he found it, without candy wrappers on the rug and Coke bottles on the piano.
6. Keep out of the parents' stuff.
7. Let the agency know as soon as possible if he can't sit as planned.

I understand that I am an employee of the agency, and I will pay 25¢ for each job that it gets for me. I also understand that if I fail to obey the rules of the contract, my name will be removed from their register.

Sitter's signature ________________

The second contract read:

II

Parents are expected to:

1. Be home at the agreed time.
2. Require no housecleaning or dishwashing.
3. Leave a list of phone numbers in case of emergency.
4. Tell their kid that they are leaving and not just sneak out the door.
5. Drive the sitter home afterwards.
6. Pay the sitter $1 per hour, $2 after midnight.
7. Call the agency as soon as possible if they discover they will not be going out after all.

We understand that we are clients of the agency and will not contact agency sitters on our own. We will pay the agency 25¢ each time a sitter is provided for us, and we further understand that if we do not obey the rules of the contract, our name will be removed from the register.

Parents' signature ________________

It took a long time to write the contracts. The wording had to be just right, and Mrs. Anselmino and Roger helped cross out and rewrite until everyone was satisfied that the contracts said what they were supposed to say.

"What will you do if a sitter gets sick at the last minute?" Elizabeth asked Eddie.

"We'll have a backup crew for emergencies."

"You don't mean . . . ?"

"You got it," said Eddie. "The three of us."

THE LAST THING they had to decide on was a name. Eddie thought that the E.E.D. Sitting Service was a good one; Dink liked the Acme Sitters Agency.

"We might even decide to expand," Eddie told them. "We could send a whole crew out to help with kids' birthday parties, for example. They could blow up the balloons, push the kids on the swings, help serve the ice cream and cake, mop up afterwards . . . Or maybe we could have a pet and plant sitting service too—like when people go on vacation and need somebody to feed the dog or water the plants while they're gone. Why, there's no end to the services we could provide."

Elizabeth was watching him from across the room. Her blue-tinted glasses were pushed up on her head, and she looked very thoughtful.

"You know," she said, "if it weren't for Eddie's ideas, we wouldn't even be having this conversation. We wouldn't even have the money to make copies of the contracts. We're all partners, I know, but it's really Eddie's business, and I think we should call it 'Eddie, Incorporated,' because nobody knows what he'll think of next. Whatever it is, the name will fit."

So Eddie, Incorporated it was, and the name and phone number went at the top of both contracts.

Between them, they had seven dollars and fifty cents from Sixth Grade Sing Day. They gave the fifty cents to Joseph to type up the contracts, and used the seven dollars to make seventy copies of them—thirty-five of each.

As the papers piled up higher and higher on the copying machine at the library, people began coming over to see what was going on.

"*Now* what are you up to?" said the head librarian, and she read copies of the contracts. "Say, this sounds pretty good! Why don't you tack an announcement up on our community bulletin board?"

Parents stopped by and looked over the contracts as the stack of papers grew even higher.

"How can we sign up for this?" they wanted to know.

Elizabeth took down their names as Dink went back and forth to the desk for change and Eddie continued to run off copies. They had eleven names before they even left the library.

That afternoon they began a tour of the neighborhood, knocking on doors and explaining the contracts.

"Does it cost anything to register with you?" people wanted to know.

"Only a dime to pay for the contract," Eddie would tell them, and if they were interested, they would sign it, with Eddie as a witness. Then he would write down their name, address, and phone number on his roster. Even the parents of Herman the Terrible—the big bad baby over on Locust Street—signed up.

Parents of toddlers, parents of twins—they all wanted their names on the register.

Meanwhile Dink and Elizabeth were going around to the homes of their friends, explaining the service to them. By seven that evening, when they met once more at the mailbox on the corner, Eddie had the names of twenty-two parents and Dink and Elizabeth had fourteen sitters. Each had paid a dime for the contract, so there was already three dollars and sixty cents in the cash box. And when they finally got back to Eddie's house, Mrs. Anselmino was waiting for them on the porch.

"The phone's been ringing all afternoon," she said. "I've got nine parents who want a sitter for next Saturday night, and I told them you'd call back."

THE BUSINESS GREW STEADILY. Each week there were more calls from people who had seen the announcement at the library or who had heard about Eddie, Incorporated from someone else.

As soon as a call came in, Eddie would take down the information and begin calling his list of sitters to see who could take the job. He would call the parents back to tell them whom to expect, and then the name would be written down in his notebook. When the sitting job was over, Dink would go collect a quarter from the parents the next morning, and Elizabeth would collect a quarter from the sitter. The fifty cents would go into the cash box in Eddie's basement, and at the end of each week, they would divide the money between them.

The first week they made about seven dollars altogether, and the next week nine. Sometimes there would be a little less money, sometimes a little more, and sometimes they would have to use some of the profits to make more copies of the contracts. But they always made a profit. They could always count on something. It was a steady business they could depend on, and growing every week. Already parents were asking for sitters for New Year's Eve, and one woman wanted to know if the agency would feed her goldfish when she went to Florida over Christmas.

Parents liked the agency because they did not have to worry that their sitter might get sick at the last minute and ruin their plans. They knew that if that happened, the agency would send somebody else.

Sitters liked the agency because they knew that if a big party came up suddenly and they had already promised to babysit, the agency would find someone to take their place. Both parents and sitters liked the agency because they knew that the other person had read the contract and would obey the rules.

Occasionally a sitter's name was removed from the register because there seemed to be too many parties and the sitter was never available. And sometimes parents were taken off the list because they continued to come home much later than they had promised. But not only was Eddie, Incorporated successful, it was becoming well known in the neighborhood.

In fact, Eddie had been so busy making phone calls that he almost forgot his own birthday. It wasn't until he saw the three-layer cake on the table one night in November that he realized he was now twelve.

The family had not forgotten, however. As butter pecan ice cream dribbled off Eddie's chin and he stuffed the last bite of fudge cake in his mouth, his mother pushed a present across the table toward him. "Open it, Eddie," she said. "I can't wait any longer."

Off came the red and white ribbons and inside was an engagement calendar for the coming year. Every day had its own page with lines for job assignments and telephone numbers. On the front was a photograph of a flock of geese flying south against a winter sunset. It looked very much like the calendar on Mr. Fowler's desk at school.

"This is great, Mom!" Eddie said delightedly. "I really mean it."

Mr. Anselmino's gift was next. It was a clothbound record book with blue columns for income and red columns for expenses, just like the one at the Anselmino Produce Store.

"I love it!" said Eddie.

"My present is sort of a surprise," said Roger. "You've got to go down in the basement to see it."

So Eddie, with his family trailing behind him went down the basement stairs. There, on the card table desk, was a bright orange extension phone.

"Oh, wow!" Eddie yelled. "I can't believe this! I can't!"

Roger was smiling broadly. "Well, it was a little more than I'd planned to spend, but I got a raise last week, so I thought, 'What the heck.' "

Eddie stood and stared. They knew now that he wasn't just playing. Nobody had his own extension phone just to mess around. Nobody had an engagement calendar for the coming year if he was expected to go out of business in a week. Nobody had a record book for expenses if he hardly made any money worth recording.

And then he remembered Joseph. Joseph hadn't come down to the basement with them. He hadn't even wished Eddie a happy birthday. In fact, as soon as the cake and ice cream had been served, Joseph had disappeared.

Maybe Eddie would never be successful as far as Joseph was concerned. Maybe he'd always be Pigfoot to his brother, the Brain. Maybe Joseph thought it was all a dumb idea and didn't want to laugh in Eddie's face.

But just then Joseph came rushing breathlessly down the basement stairs and thrust something in Eddie's hand. "I forgot to wrap it," he explained. "Sorry about the homemade card, too, but I didn't have a chance to buy one."

Eddie unfolded the card. Joseph had taken an old snapshot of Eddie and cut out his face. He'd pasted the face on a sheet of paper and then drawn Eddie's body in a business suit, sitting at a desk with a telephone in his hand. Underneath the drawing Joseph had written, "Happy Birthday to the Big Wheel."

Eddie gulped. He wasn't Pigfoot any longer. He'd graduated.

He shook the package. It was very small, very light, and for a moment, Eddie was afraid it was going to be a dumb joke—a wheel off one of his old toy trucks or something. But inside the box was a rubber stamp, and on one side were the words, "Eddie, Incorporated."

Twelve was the best time in the whole world to be alive, Eddie decided. He couldn't wait to show his presents to Dink and Elizabeth. He couldn't wait to go next door and share a piece of his cake with Mr. Clemmons. He wanted to do everything at once—talk about income tax with his parents, advertising with Roger, and investments with Joseph.

But just at that moment the bright orange telephone rang on Eddie's desk, and he answered it.

"Eddie, Incorporated," he said.

It was Janice Pringle, and her voice sounded pitifully weak. "I'm supposed to sit for the O'Conners tonight, but I think I'm catching the flu," she said. "I just can't make it."

"Don't worry," Eddie told her. "I'll find somebody else."

He hung up. It wouldn't be easy. Elizabeth was out of town on a basketball trip. Dink was at a roller skating party. Most of the other sitters were already signed up for tonight, but somebody was expected to sit with Herman the Terrible in an hour. The parents were on the register, and Eddie couldn't let them down, not even on his birthday. Business was business.

"Tell Mr. Clemmons I'll be over tomorrow with a slice of my cake," he told his family. And then, with a book for himself and a box of animal crackers for Herman, Eddie put on his jacket and went to work.

SOURCE

Newspaper

From

The New York Times

AWARD WINNING Newspaper

Students Turn Greens Into Gold

By MOLLY O'NEILL
Los Angeles

The owners of Food From the 'Hood, a produce and salad dressing company in the South Central section of Los Angeles, wear baggy, low-riding jeans, knee-length T-shirts and very big, very expensive sneakers. Many have braces on their teeth. Most have earrings in their ears. All have Attitude, and they are using it to make money and a difference in their neighborhood.

"We're hip-hop entrepreneurs," said Carlos Lopez, 15, one of the 39 students from Crenshaw High School who after the riots two years ago, turned an overgrown corner behind the school's football field into a garden and formed Food From the 'Hood to sell the vegetables and herbs they grew.

Last month, the company introduced Straight Out 'the Garden, a creamy Italian dressing. In the promotional material that the students wrote, the dressing is said to have a "kickin' taste," and "bumpin'" packaging. The dressing is already in 2,000 stores, primarily in Southern California, and it will be available nationwide within the next three months. More than 50,000 bottles of Straight Out 'the Garden have been sold, and the profits will go into a college scholarship fund for the 39 owners.

"What makes us hip is that we want to make a difference," Mr. Lopez said.

What makes them hop? Believe it or not, the students get very excited about gardening organically in raised beds on their quarter acre, selling produce at local farmers' markets, writing business plans and creating marketing campaigns. And they get even more excited talking about "line extensions" and "shelf presence."

"The uprising destroyed morale and a lot of property, and we just wanted to beautify a little corner and help feed people," said Jaynell Grayson, a 16-year-old partner in the business. "Real soon, we realized that the best way to give back to our community was to get a higher

Food From the 'Hood workers harvest vegetables from the company's garden.

education. We figured that we sell lettuce, why not sell dressing?"

None of this would have been possible without Tammy Bird, the biology teacher at Crenshaw High who created and continues to supervise the garden, and Melinda McMullen, a former public relations executive who left her job to do volunteer consulting for the group. Food From the 'Hood also got free advice from Luther, Smith & Small, a minority-owned investment banking firm in Los Angeles, which helped devise a business plan.

The students contracted with Sweet Adelaide Enterprises, a business owned by women in nearby Hawthorne, to process and bottle the dressing, and with Bromar Southern California in Anaheim to distribute the dressing.

They received other help along the way. The State of California riot recovery fund donated the $49,000 it took to teach the students basic business skills, and the Rebuild L.A. fund donated the $50,000 it took to build the company's office and develop the salad dressing.

Product development began in a blender at the 'Hood offices, and when the students had achieved the balance of basil and parsley they wanted, they worked with a food technologist to formulate their homemade dressing for mass-market production. The technologist presented six different formulas before getting a thumbs-up from Food From the 'Hood.

When word of the students' product seeped out into the secretive and competitive world of salad dressings, Norris Bernstein of Los Angeles, the founder of the Bernstein's Salad Dressing Company, volunteered to do the final work on the formula, help price the product and develop a marketing plan.

"We were like, 'It has to have basil and parsley because we're big into basil and parsley,'" said Mark Sarria, 18, the chief executive of Food From the 'Hood. "Mr. Bernstein, he listened to us; we listened to him. This is, like, the way the world is supposed to work, O.K.?"

Food From the 'Hood takes business and social policy quite seriously. After the two initial start-up grants, the company refused donations but is accepting investments under certain conditions. "Taking something for free disempowers," Mr. Sarria said. "Taking investment empowers because it means we're responsible for the payback."

Company decisions are made by consensus at Tuesday afternoon meetings. It took months to evolve a policy about dirty shoes on the new gray wall-to-wall carpeting at the corporate office, 1,000 square feet in a former storeroom behind Crenshaw High's biology classroom. The office is furnished with an imitation-marble conference table and five work stations equipped with computers that are loaded with everything from a sophisticated accounting program to S.A.T. tutorials.

"We were not into wasting it, so we had a corporate policy about shoe removal," Mr. Sarria said. "But the no-shoes thing made bad feeling, so we decided, hey, just try to wipe your feet when you come in out of the garden. Morale is more important than carpeting." (The carpeting is still spotless.)

It took even longer for the company to devise a policy for disbursing profits. After months, it was agreed that students would be awarded points during the two 20-week semesters for the hours they worked, for their grades and for receiving or providing tutoring.

The student-owners can also lose points if their grades dip, if they miss business meetings or if they behave in a manner that does not befit a Food From the 'Hood owner. Based on the company's first-quarter performance, Ms. McMullen projects that a student with three years service to the company and decent grades can earn up to a $45,000 scholarship by graduation.

At 7:15 A.M. on a Saturday morning in early June, the marketing prowess of Food From the 'Hood lacked the corporate polish of its press releases or the clean-edged imagery of its salad-dressing labels. After several hours of picking, bundling and packing herbs and lettuce, eight student-owners loaded the produce as well as salad dressing and T-shirts into beat-up cars and roared down Crenshaw Boulevard toward the freeway and the Santa Monica Farmers' Market.

"Picture this caravan steaming along toward Mrs. Gooch's in Beverly Hills," Ms. McMullen said. "I mean, here is the uppest of upscale grocers, ready to explain the retailing end of produce and dressing, and here we come."

At the farmers' market on the Third Street Promenade in Santa Monica, the owners of Food From the 'Hood donned aprons of blue and gold, Crenshaw's colors, and while local growers presided serenely over bundles of organic herbs, cottage-made goat cheese and fertilized duck eggs, they regaled shoppers.

"Tasty and good, it's food from the 'hood" was Mr. Sarria's rap. "T-shirts here. You're very near. Get them now. Later won't be any no how."

Money, herbs, lettuce, dressing and T-shirts changed hands. The owners of Food From the 'Hood see these as so many transactions in a changing world order. Between sales, they discussed the future.

"My experience designing the label made me see that I wanted to be an art director for an advertising agency," said Ben Osborne, 16.

Mr. Sarria, who has been scouted by three major league teams, said: "I'm going to play baseball for a few years. But I'm headed for international business. My family's from Nicaragua."

Sunflowers brighten up the garden—and their seeds can be sold, too.

Ms. Grayson is less sure about her future. She has to take three buses to get from her grandfather's house in the Watts section to Crenshaw, but she has a straight–A average, works at a part-time job bagging groceries at a supermarket and works, as do most Food From the 'Hood owners, 20 hours a week on the enterprise. She had always thought she'd be a brain surgeon. But two years ago, she became an "O.G."

"That means Original Gangster on the streets, but here it means Original Gardener," she said. "Working here, I found out that I love business. I love the invoices, the budgeting, the planning, collecting the money. O.K., I'm a Renaissance woman. I love science. I love business. I'm not sure at the present how I can combine the two."

SOURCE

FOOD FROM THE 'HOOD™

Press Release

FOOD FROM THE 'HOOD™

a natural food products company

Seak Chan *Age 16*

About Our Company Name...

Many people have asked us how we came up with the name Food From the 'Hood. The answer is simple: we named our company the same way other businesses name their companies. In September 1992, we had a series of meetings to discuss what qualities we wanted to communicate about our company and how we wanted to position ourselves with our customers.

We identified four main qualities we wanted people to know about us:

- **We are a student-owned business.** That meant our name had to be simple and fun. We didn't want to come across like a big corporation.
- **We're in the food business.** Our original product line was organic produce, but we wanted our company name to leave room for growth.
- **We're headquartered in the inner-city.** There aren't enough companies headquartered in the inner city. We wanted people to know that we're proud to be here.
- **We are a multi-cultural company.** Our company is 85% African-American, 13% Latino and 2% Asian-American. We wanted people to know that we respect and appreciate all people.

After identifying our primary qualities, we brainstormed a list of possible names on a blackboard. After two-and-a-half hours, we had 72 names. Some were funny, some were smart, some were terrible! We narrowed our list down to five "finalists" and then set about testing them with different people.

Carlos Lopez *Age 16*

Osofu Washington *Age 17*

We didn't use a real formal process to test our possible company names—we just went out and talked to everyone we could find. Our adult advisors and parents helped, too, by interviewing people they worked with. At the end of two weeks, we had talked with people who worked downtown, uptown and in the middle of town! We talked with people of all races, colors and creeds. We talked with doctors, homemakers, lawyers, advertising executives, shop owners, etc.

Almost everyone we spoke with—from Santa Monica to Santa Ana—voted for Food From the 'Hood. (Straight Out 'the Garden—the name we are now using for our salad dressing—came in second.)

People said the name Food From the 'Hood identified our product line (food) and told people where we are located (the 'hood, which is short for "inner city neighborhood").

We did have some concern about the reference to "'hood," but people said it was creative, positive and fun—especially after we came up with the colorful lettering of our name.

We were also concerned that people wouldn't understand that we are multi-cultural—but once we designed our company logo (which features two hands from two different cultures), that problem was solved.

Once we went public with Food From the 'Hood, we knew we had a hit on our hands. People usually smile or laugh when they hear our company name. And they never forget us.

When it comes down to it, those are the qualities most professionals look for in a company name.

This backgrounder by Ivan Lopez
Student-owner

Kristi Hernandez
Age 17

SOURCE

Article

IN 1853, LEVI STRAUSS MADE AND SOLD THE FIRST PAIR OF JEANS—BY HIMSELF. SINCE THEN, JEANS HAVE BECOME BIG BUSINESS. A WHOLE TEAM NOW WORKS TOGETHER TO GET YOUR JEANS TO YOUR LOCAL STORE. COME MEET THE MEMBERS OF...

THE JEANS TEAM

BY NANCY FITZGERALD

You head for the mall with money in your pocket, thinking about a new pair of jeans. As you look through the racks, you get the feeling that somebody's been reading your mind. How did they know the exact type of jeans you wanted? Has somebody been intercepting your brain waves?

Actually, yes. Before the teams of workers who get *your* favorite brand of jeans to the store stonewash a single yard of denim, they find out exactly what kind of jeans you're looking for. Then they make them for you. That makes you the first—and the last—person on the team.

HERE'S HOW IT WORKS.

The Merchandisers

The merchandisers' job is to make sure that people will buy the jeans. How do they do that? "We start with market research," says Joe Bugni, assistant product manager for juniors at Lee Jeans. "We keep our eyes open to see what people are wearing. We check out the big stores in New York and L.A. to see what the competition is selling. And we also travel to schools and colleges to set up meetings to find out from young people what they want." At these meetings, known as *focus groups*, the merchandiser brings along many different styles of jeans. The teens in the group look the items over, try them on, and talk about how the jeans look and feel. "Young people's opinions are very important to merchandisers," Joe Bugni says.

When Joe gets back to his office—or even while he's still on the plane—he makes sketches of jeans he thinks customers will want. He'll add notes about fit or color or fabric treatment: Should jeans be stonewashed, or dyed purple, or left dark blue? When he's done, he meets with a designer to discuss his ideas.

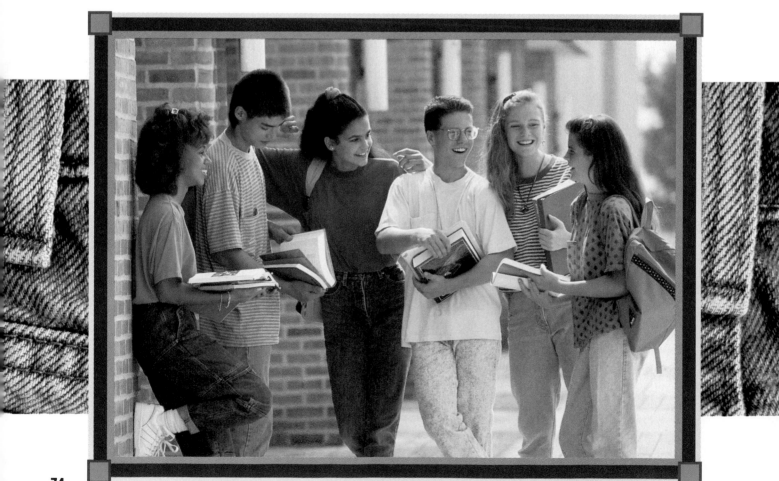

The Design Team

Although the designer will have the merchandiser's sketches and notes in hand, he or she still has to make many decisions about the new jeans. Sometimes, the designer will meet with a production team to review the new ideas. "We might want to add something to the jeans, like flannel knee patches," says Courtney Connor, a design director for Gitano jeans. "But we can't add too much, because that would make the jeans too expensive for our customers. So we sit and discuss our ideas." By the end of the meeting, the group will have decided on everything from the fabric to the type of thread to the kinds of stitching.

Once all the information is gathered, it's time to make the pattern for the jeans. At Lee, the designer gathers all the information—are the jeans baggy or tapered? do they have four pockets or five?—and plugs it into a computer. When all the details are worked out, the computer spits out a paper pattern. Then it's off to the cutting table.

The Experimental Sewers

After the fabric is cut by a computer according to the pattern, it goes to the experimental sewing department. About 25 top-flight sewers stitch it up and fit it on a dummy. But the end product is not always perfect. The right leg may be shorter than the left, or the back pockets may be too small. If this happens, the designer heads back to the computer to work out the kinks.

The Models

When all the problems are worked out, the jeans are sewn up and fit on real people. It's a good idea for companies to keep the same models on the payroll as long as possible so there will be a consistent fit.

They all fit? Great! Now the designer takes the finished product to the boss for approval.

The Sewing Team

After the product has been approved, paper patterns in all sizes go back to the sewers. They whip up a small run of jeans in different sizes for test marketing.

Jeans Time Line

The styles might have changed over the past 150 years or so, but one thing has remained the same--denim!

1850
Levi Strauss bursts onto the jeans scene by inventing the first pair of jeans--and the riveted pocket--for the San Francisco gold rush miners.
1860
Ride 'em Cowboy! In the wild west, cowboys start wearing jeans.
1900
More and more people move to cities--and factory workers decide that jeans are the most comfortable thing to wear to work.

THE MARKETERS

The test jeans go out to stores in different parts of the country. Then the marketers keep their fingers crossed and hope their jeans are a winner. If the sales are hot, then the jeans are rolled out.

When the manufacturers decide to "roll out," or mass produce, a new style of jeans, they have to let customers know about them. So the marketers meet with the merchandisers and the people from sales to come up with an advertising plan.

At this meeting they figure out who's going to be buying the jeans —teenage girls? college students? moms and dads? Then they have to plan an advertising campaign that will attract that group to their jeans.

"We come up with a rough idea for a campaign in the form of a drawing," says Pam Breeman, vice president of marketing and advertising at Gitano. "When we were planning advertising for our kids' jeans, for instance, we realized that the environment is very important to young people. So we designed the big signs and size charts you see in the store on recycled brown craft paper."

1940
World War II breaks out and high waisted button-fly jeans become the official uniform of the U.S. Navy and Coast Guard.

On the home front, Rosie the Riveter and countless other women defense workers start wearing jean-style work pants.

1950
Young people start imitating actors Marlon Brando and James Dean by wearing straight-legged jeans with black leather jackets.

The Ad Agency

Then the company calls in an ad agency to create finished ads for magazines, newspapers, TV, and billboards. Getting an ad campaign ready takes at least three months, and the ads must be completed by the time the jeans hit the store. But before any ads run, consumer researchers will show them to groups of people to make sure they're sending the right message. What have consumers learned from the ads? Do the ads make them want to try the jeans? Sometimes what the researchers learn results in a small change in the jeans.

Once Again the Sewers

Now it's time to gear up for mass production. The designers send their patterns to the manufacturing plants. After any production problems are worked out, the sewers make the "sell-sample" cut—about 250 pairs of jeans. Then the jeans go out for processing, such as bleaching or dying. Afterward, they're boxed for salespeople to show to department store buyers across the country.

1960
Hippies think jeans are neat to wear, and they begin to embroider and patch their old jeans. They also decorate bell-bottom jeans with rhinestones, paint, and nailheads.
Teens spend hours bending over bathtubs trying to prewash and bleach their jeans.
1970
Prewashed jeans hit the market (and teens breathe a sigh of relief that they won't have to bend over their bathtubs anymore)!

THE SALES TEAM

The jeans company now has to persuade retail stores around the country to sell their jeans. At Lee, the sales force goes out with sample jeans to show the "line" to department stores, boutiques, and discount stores. Each salesperson has his or her own territory. One may concentrate on the Midwest, while another focuses only on California.

Things work a little differently at Gitano. They send an entire team to each store to meet with the store buyers. "We send out somebody from sales, merchandising, design, and marketing," says Pam Breeman.

"Each person has a different area of expertise. The designer, for example, can talk about the hot new trends, and the marketing person can explain our advertising plans. It's much more efficient to work together."

THE STORE BUYERS

Every store, from the small boutique to the large department store chain, has buyers who choose the items it will offer for sale. Once the buyers decide which jeans the store's customers will like, they send the orders to the manufacturer's customer-service department.

1980
Tight-fitting jeans become the craze when jeans companies start offering peg-leg, spandex, and zip-ankle styles.

Stone-washed jeans hit the market.

1990
Hip-hop musicians start the craze for baggy jeans, which are sometimes worn backwards!

No, it's not a defect-- stores begin to sell jeans with holes thanks to the "grunge" look.

Customer-Service Department

When the customer-service people get the order, they contact the distribution center, where the jeans are stored.

The Warehouse Workers

When an order comes in at the distribution center, it's time for the workers to get busy. They pull the jeans from big bins marked by style, size, and color. Then the jeans are sent for "special operations" such as ticketing. Finally, workers pack the jeans in boxes, load them onto a truck, and send them to the store.

The Salesclerk

Once the jeans arrive at the store, they make one final trip—to the selling floor. Once there, they have to look good enough to attract *your* attention. Some stores, like The Gap, put a lot of effort into how their jeans are displayed. They think jeans will sell better if they are in large, neat stacks. That's where the salesclerks come in. Part of their job is to keep the jeans looking neat in their display. "On a busy Saturday, I probably fold 200 pairs of jeans," says Gap salesclerk, Mary Lorrain.

Jeans have become big business in the United States. How big? *Very* big! In 1992 there were 67 brands of jeans on the market. Over 400,000,000 pairs of jeans were sold, at a total cost of $4,752,960,000!

You

Once you've picked the jeans you want, the salesclerk takes your money and enters the purchase into the store's computer. Making this purchase is like casting your vote for your favorite pair of jeans. The store will use the sales numbers to keep track of which jeans are popular and should be reordered. You can bet that back at the manufacturing company, someone in merchandising will be checking those numbers, too, to find out what kinds of jeans to make next.

The jeans business has grown a lot more complicated since Levi Strauss made and sold that very first pair. But don't worry. The jeans team will keep them coming.

SUPER SALES

All those jeans sales certainly add up! Check out the graph below to see how many millions of pairs have been sold.

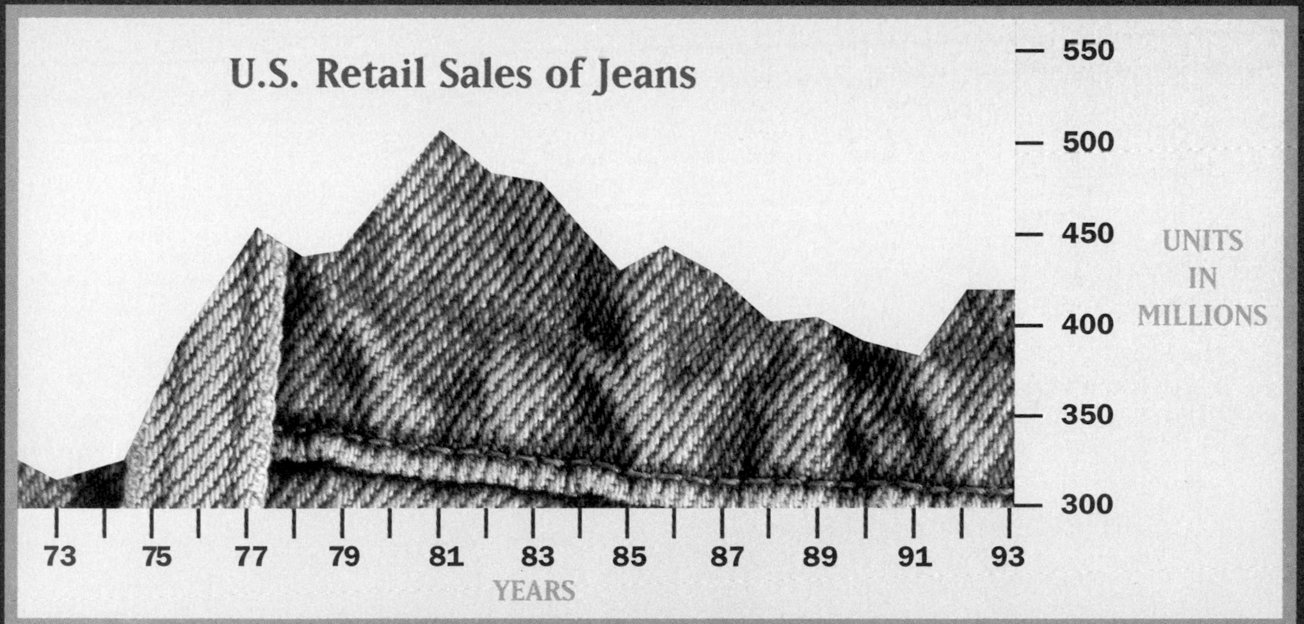

Source: MRCA Information Services, Inc.

SOURCE

the history magazine for young people

COBBLESTONE®

Magazine

AWARD WINNING

Magazine

LEVI'S GOLD

by Dorothy Slate

When the clipper ship sailed through California's Golden Gate that March day in 1853, twenty-four-year-old Levi Strauss rushed to the deck, eager to see San Francisco. The Gold Rush, started in 1848, still drew men by the thousands to seek their fortunes. Strauss was one of them.

Six years earlier, he had left Bavaria in Germany to escape unfair laws against Jews and to join his older brothers Jonas and Louis in New York. They taught him English and told him peddling was an honorable occupation in the United States. Now he faced a new challenge. In his baggage were goods to sell. His brothers had helped select them in New York before he left on his long voyage around Cape Horn to California. Gold miners were sure to need thread, needles, scissors, thimbles, and rolls of canvas cloth for tents and wagon covers.

As Strauss looked toward the city, he saw several small boats approaching the ship. When they came close, some of their passengers clamored for news from the East. Others climbed aboard to see what merchandise the ship had brought. In a short while, Strauss had sold almost everything he had brought with him. Only the rolls of canvas remained.

Stepping ashore, he saw a bustling city with many "stores" that were merely tents or shanties.

With gold dust from his sales aboard ship, Strauss bought a cart.

He loaded his rolls of canvas and pushed the cart along wood-planked sidewalks. He parked on Montgomery Street, waiting for miners to pass by.

A prospector stopped to look at his canvas.

"It's for tenting," Strauss explained.

"Shoulda brought pants," the prospector told him. "Pants don't wear worth a hoot in the diggin's. Can't get a pair strong enough to last."

Instantly, the young entrepreneur sought out a tailor and created the first pair of jeans. Pleased with them, his customer later strutted around San Francisco. "Doggone, if a man ever had a pair of pants strong as Levi's before," he said.

The demand for "Levi's" grew so fast that Strauss could hardly keep up with it. When the brown canvas was gone, he switched to a sturdy fabric, *serge de Nimes*. The name was quickly shortened to "denim," and Strauss adopted the indigo blue familiar today.

Levi's brothers Jonas and Louis were his partners, as was David Stern, who had married Levi's sister, Fanny. They decided to call their firm Levi Strauss & Company, agreeing that Levi was the "business head" in the family. Years went by, and the business grew.

Then, in July 1872, a letter arrived from Jacob W. Davis, a tailor in Reno. The letter explained that he was now reinforcing pants pocket corners with copper rivets. Rivets strengthened the seams, which tore out when miners and other workers stuffed their pockets with gold nuggets and tools.

Davis was flooded with orders but worried that someone would steal his idea. If Levi Strauss & Company would take out a patent in his name, Davis would give them half the right to sell the riveted clothing.

Strauss immediately saw the profit potential. Instead of nine or ten dollars a dozen, the riveted pants could bring thirty-six dollars—just for adding a penny's worth of metal. It was a good risk.

The U.S. Patent Office took its time in granting Strauss a patent. It took ten months and many revisions and amendments before the Patent Office agreed that the idea of riveted pockets was unusual enough to be patented.

When Davis moved his family to San Francisco, Strauss put him in charge of production. Soon a force of sixty women stitched Levi's on a piecework basis. The orange thread still used today was an attempt to match the copper rivets. Another still-used trademark is the leather label featuring two teamsters whipping a pair of horses trying to tear apart the riveted pants.

Levi Strauss found gold not in streams or mines, but in fulfilling an everyday need. Today presidents, movie stars, and millions of other people wear Levi's and other brands of jeans, clothing created by an entrepreneur who responded to the needs of the market.

WORKSHOP 2

How to

Make an Organizational Chart

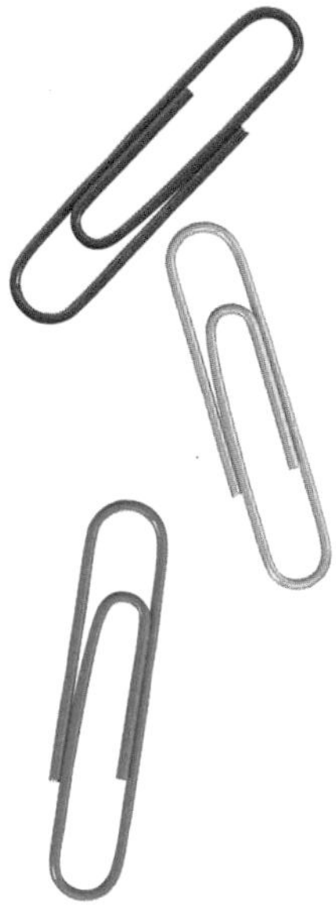

To run a successful business, an entrepreneur must make sure that all the work gets done–and that it gets done as smoothly and efficiently as possible. Making an organizational chart is one way to keep track of who does what and how employees work together.

What is an organizational chart? An organizational chart lists each job involved in operating a business. The chart also shows how the employees who fill those jobs interact with one another.

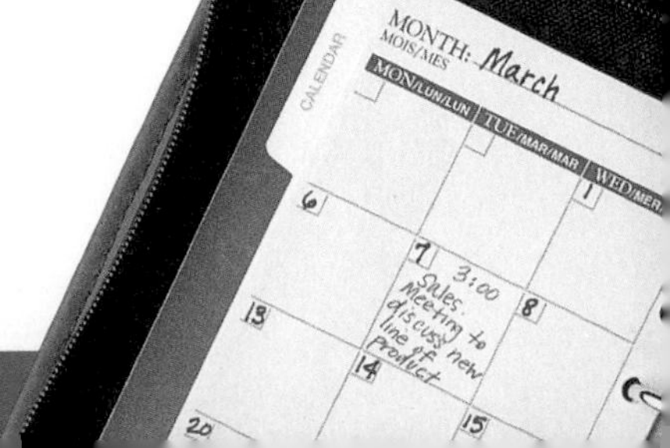

Tom's of Maine Organizational Chart

The organizational chart provides the job titles of the people who work in the business.

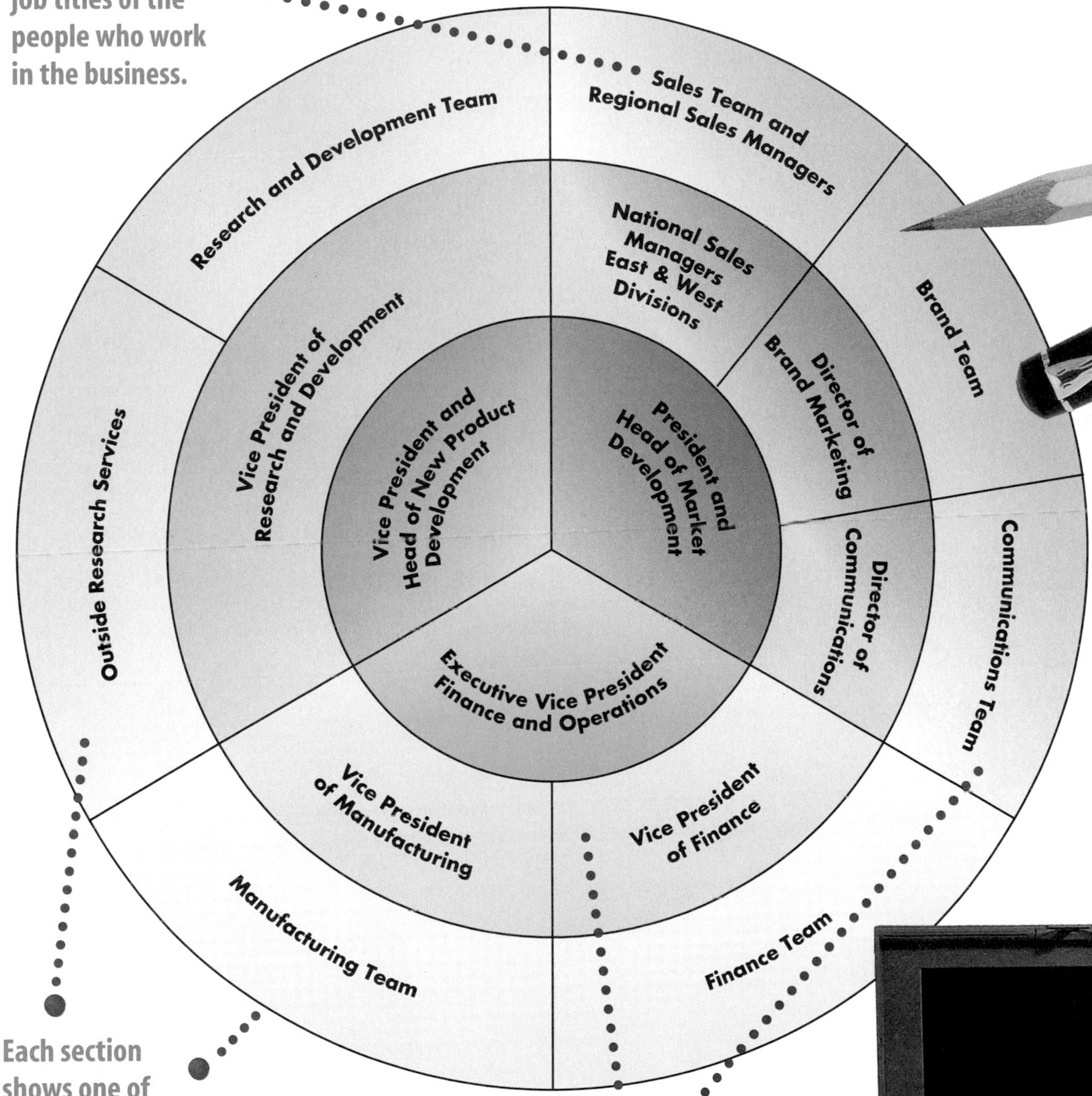

Each section shows one of the divisions in the company.

Colors help identify the different divisions.

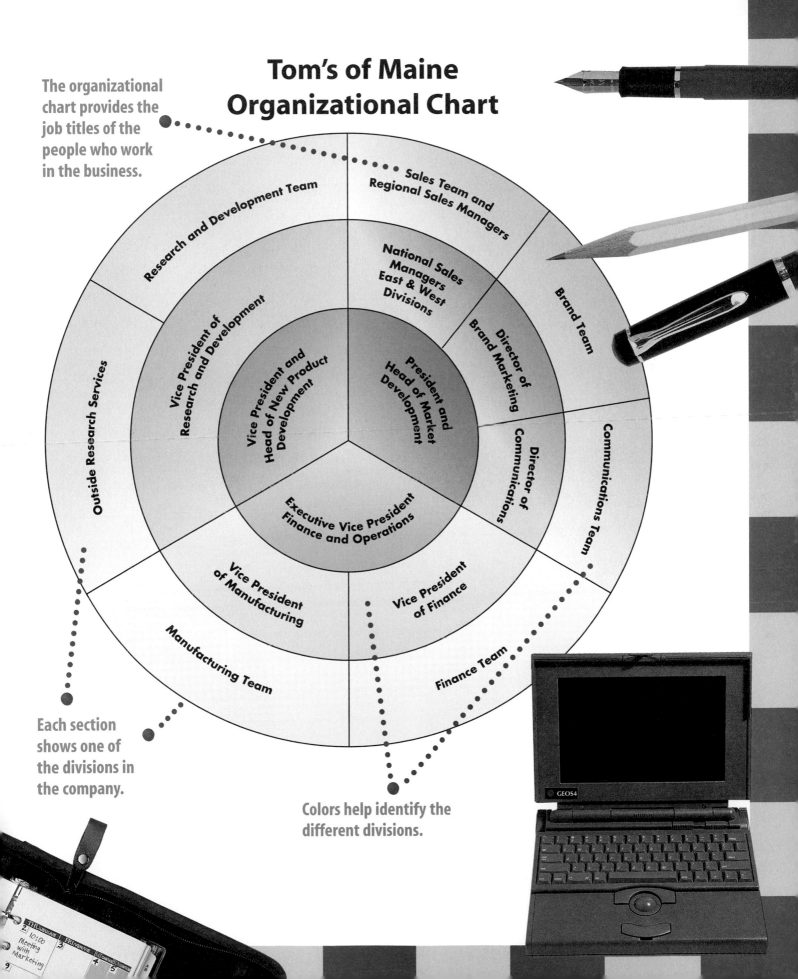

1 Choose a Business

What kind of business interests you? a magazine? a bakery? a sporting goods store? a video rental shop? With your group, make a list of businesses you know. If you're stuck for an idea, think about how your own school cafeteria is run. As a group, agree on which business to study.

TOOLS

- notebook and pencil
- scrap paper
- chart paper or posterboard
- ruler
- markers

2 Do Research

Study your business. Find out everything you can about how it is run. How many departments does the business include? How many people work in each department? What does each employee do? How do the different people and departments work together? In order to find out how the people in a business work together as a team, your group members need to work as a team, too! Decide how to gather information. Divide up the research work. Each team member might talk to a different worker. Also, you might make a team visit to the business to observe it in operation.

3 Create Your Chart

Once you have the information you need, talk about what your chart will include and how the information will be organized. Not all businesses are set up the same way, so choose a layout that fits the business you've studied. Use your notebook or scrap paper to make rough sketches of possible designs. Choose the design that works best, and copy it onto posterboard. Don't forget to plan your descriptions as carefully as you plan the design!

Tip Experiment with different shapes for your organizational chart. Try a pyramid. Try a web. What about a figure eight?

4 Present Your Chart

As a group, look over your chart and talk about the different roles people play in the business. If your group had to run this business, who do you think would do each job? Which job might suit you? After you've discussed your chart, show it to other groups. Have each member of your team play the role of someone in the organizational chart and tell a little about his or her job.

If You Are Using a Computer . . .

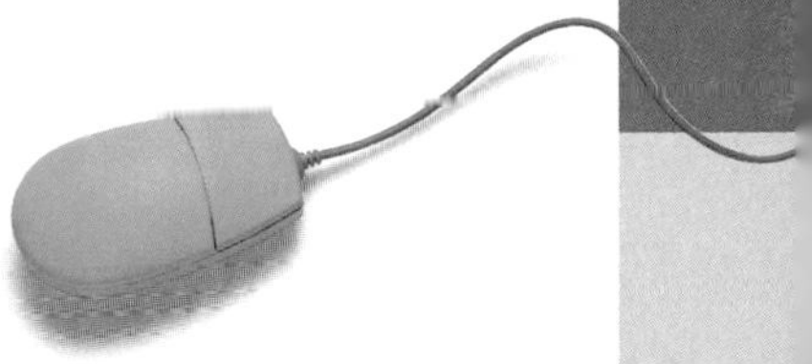

Create your organizational chart on the computer by using the Poster format. Use drawing tools to make symbols for your chart.

THINK

How many people on your chart are in a position to supervise others? What kind of skills do you think they need?

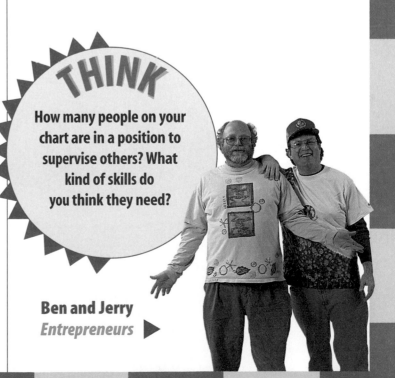

Ben and Jerry
Entrepreneurs

IP
ORDER BOARD
IP
IP
INTERGALACTIC PIZZA
FREE DELIVERY FREE DELIVERY FREE DELIVERY FREE DELIVERY

SECTION 3

Business must adapt to changing conditions.

Changing With the Times

Meet a farm family that knows how to keep in step with the times. Read a poem about farming in the U.S.A.

Follow the Skinner family as they try to get their new business off the ground. Get the facts about the service industry from a series of graphs.

PROJECT

Write a plan that will get your business up and running.

SOURCE

Photo Essay

THE ADAMSES

AWARD WINNING Photographer

A Photo Essay by
GEORGE ANCONA

Text by
JOAN ANDERSON

Willie Adams's house and farm in Greensboro, Georgia, are tucked away behind the towering pines that line the east Georgia highway.

"At the fork in the road, bear left," Willie says, "and go down the hill and over a bridge. You'll see our sign. The house is at the end of the road."

Willie lives with his wife, Linda, daughter, Shonda, son, Cedric, and his mother, Rosie.

OF GEORGIA

From
THE AMERICAN FAMILY FARM

"I spent my childhood following my grandfather as he steered the horse-drawn plow and worked these ninety-two acres," Willie says. "In those days, the fields around here were full of cotton, peanuts, and corn."

Despite hard times, Willie's grandfather did whatever was necessary to hold onto the land.

"Then, when I was just fifteen, he took ill and could no longer work," Willie remembers, "and things had to change if the farm was to survive."

"That's how I eventually got into chicken farming," he says. "There was no way I could manage growing crops and go to school at the same time. Besides, with synthetic fiber becoming more and more popular, cotton was on its way out. My mother and I were forced to change our way of farming altogether."

They phased out crops and began raising beef cattle, improving their pastureland to allow them to feed the new herd. Twelve years ago, Willie added two poultry houses to his farm: "In this business you always have to look ahead to what will sell. Poultry farming doesn't depend on weather, because the chickens are kept in specially built houses. As long as they are fed properly, you're pretty much guaranteed a healthy chicken at the end of eight weeks."

"We live a simple life—real quiet and peaceful," says Rosie, sitting on the porch with her grandchildren on her lap. "There's always a breeze on this front porch, because the house sits on a little knoll and catches the air."

"It sure is a perfect place to raise children. Lets 'em see down-to-earth living. That way they learn how things are. Living on a farm allows you to go down to grass roots and know that something can always be created from the soil."

Every day, Cedric sets off for the fields with his red wagon.

"He collects whatever is growing out there," his grandmother says. "Willie did the same thing when he was little, and look what happened to him!"

Everyone has a place here. Linda Adams tends to the poultry houses when her husband is off in the fields. In the afternoon she says good-bye to the children and goes to work in a nearby sock factory.

"Most of the women out here work away from the farm at least part time," she says. "It adds a steady income for us, along with what we get from the chickens. If farming is in your blood and you want to stay on the land, you do what needs to be done to make that possible."

Twice daily, Willie drives five miles in his pickup truck to a tract of U.S. Forest pastureland where his seventy Beefmaster cattle graze. "I rent the land for a small fee," he says. "It's one way the government is trying to help the small farmer."

"Here in Georgia the cattle can stay out all year long," Willie says as he unloads buckets of feed. "They're good animals. I wouldn't feel like a farmer if I didn't have a herd of cows."

"A few years back something very exciting happened to me," says Willie. "I began meeting other black farmers who seemed to love agriculture as much as I did. At the time, we were all struggling, working independently of each other. Most of our wives had jobs, and none of us could afford hired hands. Gradually it occurred to me that perhaps we could help each other, that surely there would be strength in our combined ideas. And so I formed a cooperative in which the members would experience a sense of kinship, share knowledge and labor from time to time, and offer each other moral support— just like it would be if we were brothers working the same farm. The co-op is like an extended family farm."

Today ten members, all of whom share common roots, belong to the cooperative. They are Willie and Linda Adams, I.V. and Annie Henry, Leroy Cooper, Melvin Cunningham, Roger Lemar, Frank Smith, Robert Williams, and Mrs. E.M. Neal.

Descended from Africans brought as slaves to this country over one hundred years ago to till the white man's land, these fifth-generation farmers truly know the cycles of agriculture.

Willie is in constant contact with the co-op members, discussing individual needs and problems and trying to make arrangements for one farmer to help another.

"We share large machinery, trailers, and trucks for hauling livestock," he explains. "We save a lot of money by not owning identical equipment." The members are always on the lookout for used equipment that can be bought inexpensively and restored for communal use.

"Some of us are better mechanics than others," Willie says. Today he is calling Melvin Cunningham to repair his tractor, and in return for his time Melvin will use the tractor to work his land. Similarly, Willie recently borrowed a truck from one of the co-op members to pick up seeds a feed store was giving away. He managed to get enough to be able to share them all around.

The members also share animals. Willie drives twenty miles over to Oncone County to Frank Smith's farm in order to make arrangements to use his prize bull for breeding.

Frank's chicken and cattle farm is a bit smaller than the others. "I bought this land right out of high school," Frank explains. "I wasn't quite as lucky as the other members of the co-op, who inherited farmland. There was nothing for me to inherit except the wise words of my great-grandmother, who was a slave. She used to say: 'Make the best better, and then you can't go wrong.'"

Leroy Cooper, who owns the largest farm in the co-op, also lives in Oncone County. He has six poultry houses and a huge hog operation and is always looking for ways to improve his herd.

Today Leroy is showing Willie his newly built barn with special pens for nursing sows. The pens are built to confine the eight-hundred-pound mothers so they won't crush their piglets when they try to suckle.

Nearby is Leroy's son, who seems more than comfortable handling the piglets.

"I hope he'll see that this is a good life," Leroy tells Willie.

"I still dream of dairy farming," Willie says as he drives through Putnam County, the dairy county of Georgia, and pulls up to Roger Lemar's place. "It was my first goal as a child. But I soon learned it was more time-consuming than other kinds of farming because of the milking schedule."

Willie is greeted by Roger and his father, Charlie Lemar, who built their cement block milking barn back in the early fifties. Charlie Lemar taught his son the business, and Roger has expanded it threefold.

"We started with fifteen acres, and now my sixty cows graze on one hundred and thirty-five!

"Because it's been so difficult to show a profit in farming, a lot of our kids moved to the city," explains Roger. "I realized that by modernizing and expanding we might be able to reap larger profits and in doing so attract the kids back to the land. The co-op has helped by giving us access to the latest information on farm management and loan opportunities."

Willie talks milk prices and inquires about borrowing the Lemars' cattle trailer. The sweet smell of fresh milk permeates the air as ten cows at a time are led into stalls and hooked up to milker units for the second milking of the day. Contentment radiates from Roger's face as he works.

"I spent ten years away from this," he says, "and I'm glad to be back. It provides a peace of mind that I like. I don't enjoy punching a time clock and having people standing over me. Here it's just me and my father."

This being June in Georgia, it is time for the first cutting of hay. Willie is off to I.V. Henry's place, hoping that I.V., who owns the only baler in the co-op, will have time to harvest one of Willie's fields.

Willie finds his friend ready to hook the baler to his tractor, and he goes to help. I.V. then takes off across the broad field where freshly cut yellow hay waits to be gathered up into massive round bales. "Round bales can sit out in the fields longer," I.V. says, "because the hay is gathered in such a way that it is better protected from the elements. Good thing, too, because none of us has enough loft space to store the square bales, which need more protection."

“This baler is an amazing machine,” he adds, pleased to have found it secondhand. “It gathers the hay in a round formation and ties it together with twine in the process. Machines like this one make farming a whole lot easier than it was in the old days.”

I.V. Henry has been a farmer since he was ten years old. His parents separated at that time, and he had no choice but to take up the chores of his father. “I learned early on that if you could raise it you didn’t have to buy it,” he says. “Since the only income most black folks had back then came from picking cotton, we learned real quick to use our extra land to raise anything and everything we wanted to eat.”

“Even today, things aren’t that easy,” I.V. continues, running his hands through a barrel of grain. “We never know whether a bank will give us a loan or turn us down. And on top of that, there are lots of folks out there who are anxious to buy us out. With the co-op we can figure out our options better.”

Because I.V. is Willie's closest co-op neighbor, the two men frequently help each other with heavy chores. In a few weeks, I.V.'s chickens will have matured, and Willie will help him herd them into boxes on turn-over day.

"Chicken farming is a one-man job until the day we ship them out," I.V. says. "Then we need all the help we can get. After the birds are gone, the entire house must be cleaned within twenty-four hours to prepare for the new shipment of baby chicks."

Weary after a long day, I.V. pauses to reflect a moment. "You know, Booker T. Washington once said: 'No race can prosper till it learns that there is as much dignity in tilling a field as in writing a poem,' and I think he was right."

"We're out to beat the statistics that say black farmers are losing their land at a rate of 9,000 acres a week," says Willie. He and his cooperative have found a way to perpetuate a lifestyle, preserve the land of their forefathers for future generations, and prosper in the process.

SOURCE

Poem

FROM

HEARTLAND

BY DIANE SIEBERT · PAINTINGS BY WENDELL MINOR

I am the Heartland,
Great and wide.
I sing of hope.
I sing of pride.

I am the land where wheat fields grow
In golden waves that ebb and flow;
Where cornfields stretched across the plains
Lie green between the country lanes.

I am the Heartland,
Shaped and lined
By rivers, great and small, that wind
Past farms, whose barns and silos stand
Like treasures in my fertile hand.

I am the Heartland.
I can feel
Machines of iron, tools of steel,
Creating farmlands, square by square—
A quilt of life I proudly wear:

A patchwork quilt laid gently down
In hues of yellow, green, and brown
As tractors, plows, and planters go
Across my fields and, row by row,
Prepare the earth and plant the seeds
That grow to meet a nation's needs.

A patchwork quilt whose seams are etched
By miles of wood and wire stretched
Around the barns and pastures where
The smell of livestock fills the air.
These are the farms where hogs are bred,
The farms where chicks are hatched and fed;
The farms where dairy cows are raised,
The farms where cattle herds are grazed;
The farms with horses, farms with sheep—
Upon myself, all these I keep.

I am the Heartland.
On this soil
Live those who through the seasons toil:

The farmer, with his spirit strong;
The farmer, working hard and long,
A feed-and-seed-store cap in place,
Pulled down to shield a weathered face—
A face whose every crease and line
Can tell a tale, and help define
A lifetime spent beneath the sun,
A life of work that's never done.

I am the Heartland.
On these plains
Rise elevators filled with grains.
They mark the towns where people walk
To see their neighbors, just to talk;
Where farmers go to get supplies
And sit a spell to analyze
The going price of corn and beans,
The rising cost of new machines;
Where steps are meant for shelling peas,
And kids build houses in the trees.

I am the Heartland.
In my song
Are cities beating, steady, strong,
With footsteps from a million feet
And sounds of traffic in the street;
Where giant mills and stockyards sprawl,
And neon-lighted shadows fall
From windowed walls of brick that rise
Toward the clouds, to scrape the skies;
Where highways meet and rails converge;
Where farm and city rhythms merge
To form a vital bond between
The concrete and the fields of green.

I am the Heartland:
Earth and sky
And changing seasons passing by.

I feel the touch of autumn's chill,
And as its colors brightly spill
Across the land, the growing ends,

And winter, white and cold, descends
With blizzards howling as they sweep
Across me, piling snowdrifts deep.
Then days grow longer, skies turn clear,
And all the gifts of spring appear—
The young are born, the seedlings sprout;

Before me, summer stretches out
With pastures draped in lush, green grass,
And as the days of growing pass,
I feel the joy when fields of grain
Are blessed by sunlight, warmth, and rain;

For I have learned of drought and hail,
Of floods and frosts and crops that fail,
And of tornadoes as they move
In frightening paths, again to prove
That in the Heartland, on these plains,
Despite Man's power, Nature reigns.

I am the Heartland.
Smell the fields,
The rich, dark earth, and all it yields;
The air before a coming storm,
A newborn calf, so damp and warm;
The dusty grain in barns that hold
The bales of hay, all green and gold.

I am the Heartland.
Hear me speak
In voices raised by those who seek
To live their lives upon the land,
To know and love and understand
The secrets of a living earth—
Its strengths, its weaknesses, its worth;
Who, Heartland born and Heartland bred,
Possess the will to move ahead.

I am the Heartland.
I survive
To keep America, my home, alive.

SOURCE

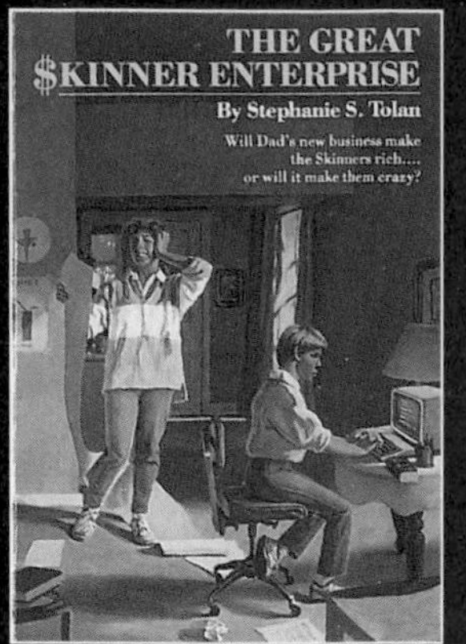

Novel

FROM

THE GREAT SKINNER ENTERPRISE

AWARD WINNING Author

BY STEPHANIE S. TOLAN

ILLUSTRATED BY HARVEY CHAN

WHEN JENNY SKINNER'S FATHER LOSES HIS JOB, HE DECIDES THAT THE FAMILY SHOULD START ITS OWN BUSINESS. AT YOUR SERVICE WILL DO ALL THE JOBS THAT PEOPLE ARE TOO BUSY TO DO FOR THEMSELVES. BUT WHEN JENNY LEARNS THAT 70 PERCENT OF SMALL BUSINESSES FAIL, SHE BEGINS TO FEEL NERVOUS. CAN AT YOUR SERVICE BE AMONG THE 30 PERCENT THAT SUCCEED?

OVER the beans and rice that night (I'd hoped Mom would take down the AUSTERITY MEASURES list when she got to be a committed partner, but she didn't) Mom and Dad talked about the CPA Mom had found that afternoon to do financial stuff for the business and the lawyer they were going to have to hire, about tax stuff they had to get done for the city and the county, and about insurance. I didn't pay much attention to any of that. But then we got to the part about who was going to do what, and I got very interested.

I seemed to be the only one in the whole family who was bothered by the flyer. Everybody else thought it was pretty and would get lots of business. Rick said he wanted to be the one who did the pet care. Marcia said she'd do the dog walking. Ben wanted to be in charge of the computer, scheduling jobs and stuff like that—and "creating the data base," whatever that meant.

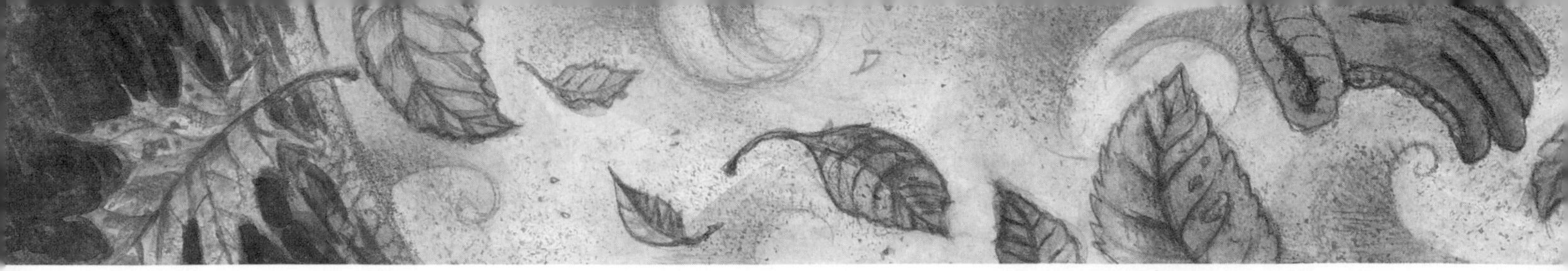

Mom said she would schedule her work days differently, since a lot of what she did she did at the library, which was open every evening. The author she worked for kept regular nine-to-five hours at his office but he didn't care if she wanted to rearrange her time, as long as she got the research he needed done in time for him to use it. She could do some of the shopping and errands At Your Service would need done in the mornings. She also said that once she learned word processing, which she ought to do anyway, she could do the letter writing. Dad said he'd take care of the lawn work. I don't think anybody noticed that I didn't volunteer for anything.

All of us had a job for the next day, though. It was Saturday, and we were all going to distribute flyers. Later, I called Sarah and asked her if she'd go with me, and she said she couldn't. It seemed awfully convenient that she'd promised to help her mother clean out their attic. For someone who liked the idea of At Your Service so well, and was so interested in getting to be an employee, she showed a decided lack of enthusiasm for the first real job, I thought.

The first problem was that the weather didn't cooperate. After weeks of unusually warm weather, we suddenly got a taste of real autumn. It was chilly. As soon as I'd finished the oatmeal Mom had made so we'd all go off fortified against the chill, I went out on the front porch to see how it really was, and decided that "chilly" wasn't entirely accurate. It was cold. And the sky was this really heavy gray and about ten feet above the roof of the house. And it was windy. September was gone, October was with us, and it felt like the middle of November.

Before she'd let us go out, Mom insisted that everybody find a winter hat—not easy in the Skinner household. Nobody could remember what they'd done with last winter's warm clothes except,

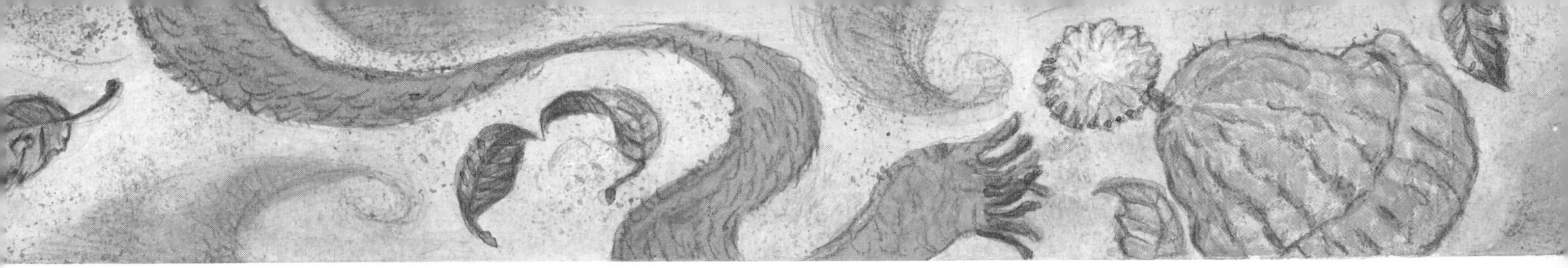

of course, Marcia, who has a place for everything and then actually keeps it there. Marcia produced two knit hats, a pair of gloves, a pair of mittens, her winter jacket (too small for her now), and a scarf. I managed to find one glove with a hole in the thumb, my jacket (also too small), and my boots (which I couldn't get my feet into anymore). Rick, after taking every single thing out of his closet and strewing everything on the floor, remembered that he'd lost his hat and mittens at the end of the winter and Mom had decided not to replace them until this year. She'd already had to buy him four hats and six pairs of mittens. Marcia loaned Rick her blue-and-white hat with the pom-pom because he refused to wear the one with the pink border. Ben hadn't had a winter hat last year because his jacket had a hood, but he came up with his baseball cap, which Mom finally accepted because it was better than nothing. I tied a red-and-white farmer's bandanna over my ears to satisfy Mom, knowing I could take it off the minute Dad dropped me off in my territory. I looked like a real geek in it. We all just wore our regular lightweight fall jackets.

Then Dad produced a huge map, on which he'd outlined each person's territory in a different color magic marker. When I pointed out that Marcia's was littler than mine, Dad said hers had more hills (though hills weren't marked on the map) and that, anyway, she was younger. I argued that eleven-year-olds have more natural energy than fifteen-year-olds, but he didn't accept that. I know it makes me sound picky and selfish to worry about whose territory was bigger, but that wasn't the real problem. I saw right away that mine included Jason Felton's house. What if he were home? I couldn't bear the thought of going up to his front door and putting a flyer through the door handle. He'd think I was using it as an excuse to come to his house. He'd think I was chasing him.

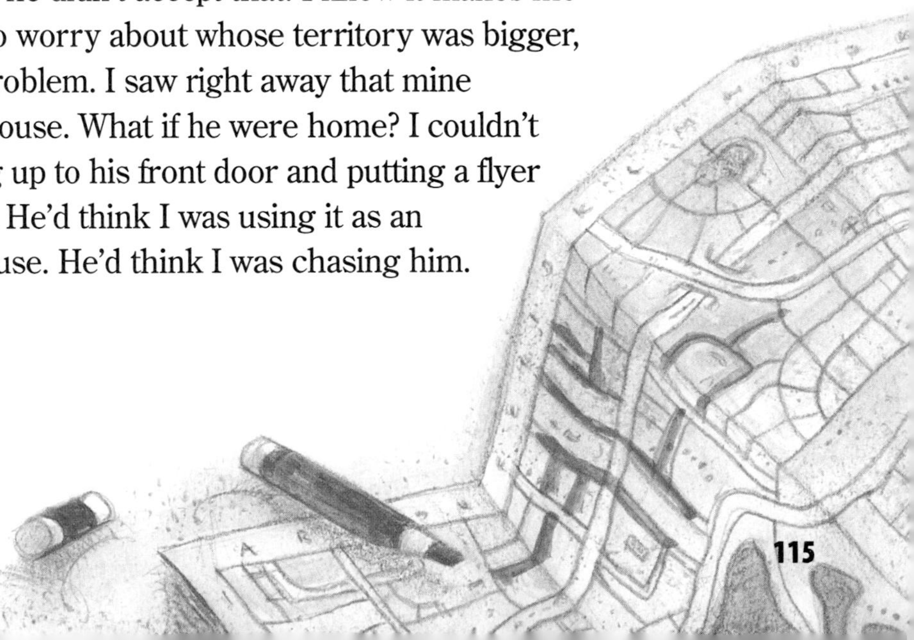

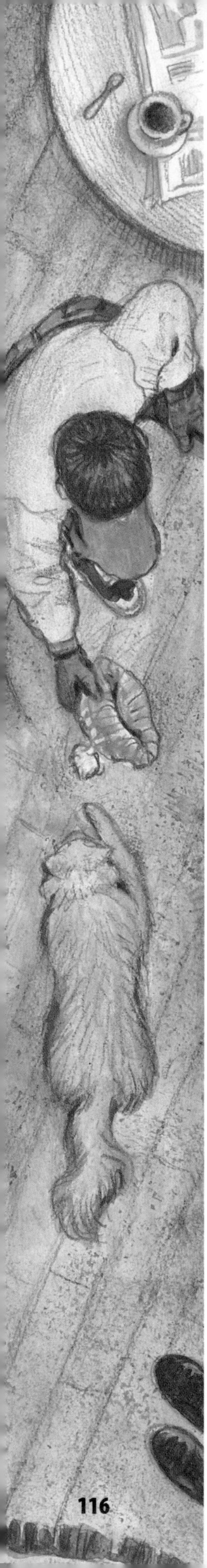

Since I couldn't get the territories switched, I decided I'd skip his block. How many customers could we miss that way, anyway? It was only one block. I knew exactly where his house was because Sarah and I had ridden our bikes past it three different times just to be sure we knew where it was. (She knew Tim Reardon's whole neighborhood practically better than she knew our own.) After showing us our territories, Dad gave each of us a piece of another map he'd cut up so that we wouldn't have to try to remember our boundaries.

While Dad was explaining to Marcia and Rick and me what to do with the flyers, and what to say if someone was outside when we delivered them (I couldn't imagine anyone being outside on a day like this, but I was glad to know what to say if someone actually saw me putting the flyer on their door), Rick was dragging Marcia's hat around him on the floor so Czar Nicholas could chase the pom-pom. Dad should have realized that Rick wasn't really listening to the instructions. He should have repeated everything especially for Rick—maybe that would have kept him from being so mad at Rick later.

Ben's territory was bigger, but that's because he was riding his bike. He was to put flyers under the windshield wipers of cars in mall and supermarket parking lots.

Finally, we were ready to go. "Okay, troops," Dad said, before we went out the front door. "This is our first mission. Remember, every person you meet is a potential customer. Smile. Be friendly and polite. If anyone has questions, do your best to answer them. If you don't know the answer, tell them to call the number on the flyer."

"You always used to tell me not to talk to strangers," Rick said.

Dad frowned. "In your territory, you're probably not going to meet many strangers, Rick. You never go farther than three blocks from home."

"But what if—"

"Okay, don't talk to strangers. All you have to do is tell them to call the number on the flyer."

"That's talking."

"So point!"

Mom took the hat from Rick's hand and pulled it down over his ears. "Why don't I go with you?"

"Oh, no! I can do my territory all by myself. I'm an officer."

"All right. Just use your head and be careful. Anyway, the *main* rule is still the same—never get into a car with a stranger."

Dad rubbed his hands. "Everybody got your flyers?"

We all nodded. Dad had tied a bundle for each of us with string so they'd be easy to carry. Ben had his in his backpack and Marcia had hers in her book bag. Rick and I were just carrying ours by the string. His was much lighter than mine, because his territory was so small.

"You all remember your instructions?" Dad asked.

We all nodded. Even Rick.

"Okay, let's roll! We'll all meet back here at"—he checked his watch—"one-thirty. That should give us plenty of time."

I'll say, I thought. Four whole hours! I could just imagine how cold my ears would get in four hours. But I didn't say anything. I was beginning to feel like a traitor. Everybody else was so gung ho!

"Let's synchronize watches," Ben suggested.

"I don't have a watch," Rick complained.

"You don't need one," Ben said. "When you're done, all you have to do is come home. You'll be the first one back."

"If everybody else gets to synchronize watches, I want to, too."

So Mom gave Rick her watch, and we all agreed it was nine thirty-four or very close to that. Mom said she'd have hot chocolate and lunch ready by one-thirty, and we set off.

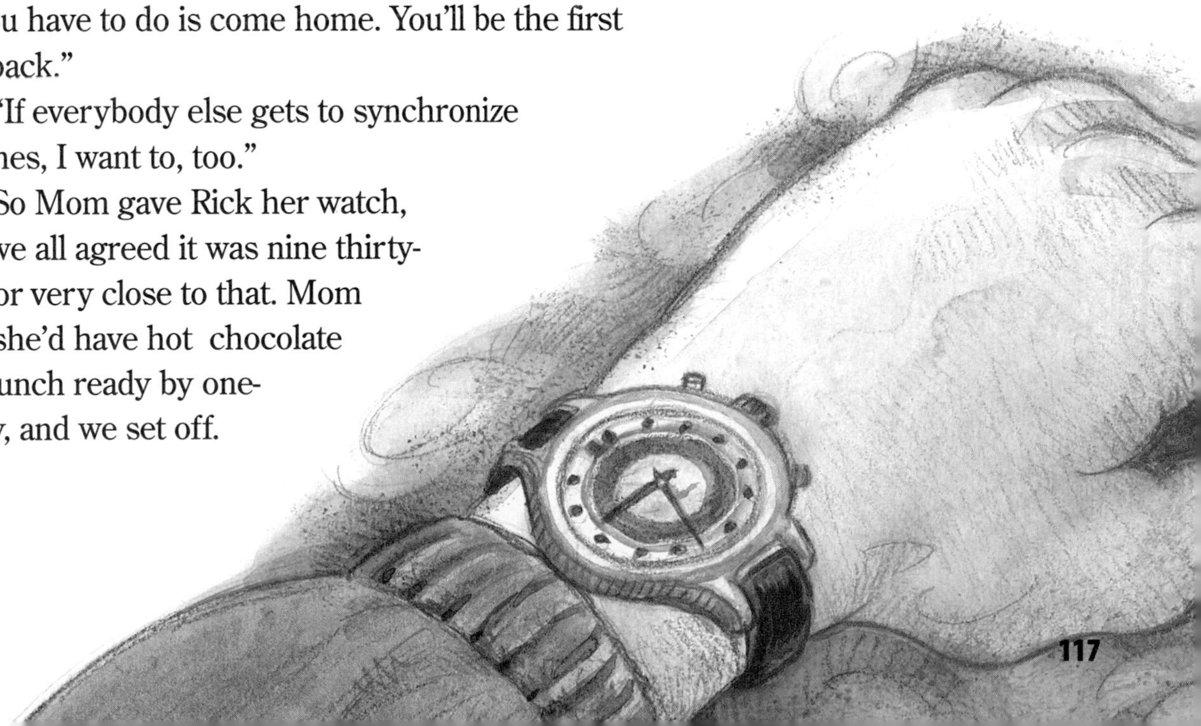

Dad dropped Marcia first, and told her to be at the same corner by five after one. Then he dropped me at the corner of Hilldale and Perry Pike. I was supposed to be back there by one-fifteen. Big as my territory was, I figured I was going to have to move pretty fast to get finished only ten minutes after Marcia. Skipping Jason's block would help.

When Dad drove away, I took off my bandanna, shoved it in my pocket, and set off. The houses on Perry Pike were pretty far apart and pretty far back from the road. It didn't take a calculator to figure out that my territory was going to turn out to be a lot bigger even than it had looked, by the time I walked up and down all those driveways. I could think of neighborhoods that would be a lot easier. But At Your Service was for people with money, and that meant big houses with big yards and long driveways. I wished Sarah were with me. Cleaning the attic was beginning to sound like a good way to spend Saturday.

At the front door of the first house, I discovered the flaw in Dad's method of bundling the flyers. They were easy enough to carry that way, but I couldn't get one out without untying the whole bundle. So I sat down on the top step and untied them, laid one down next to me, and tied the bundle again, this time with the string going around them in only one direction, so I could just slip them out, one at a time. A puff of cold wind picked up the first one and blew it back down the driveway.

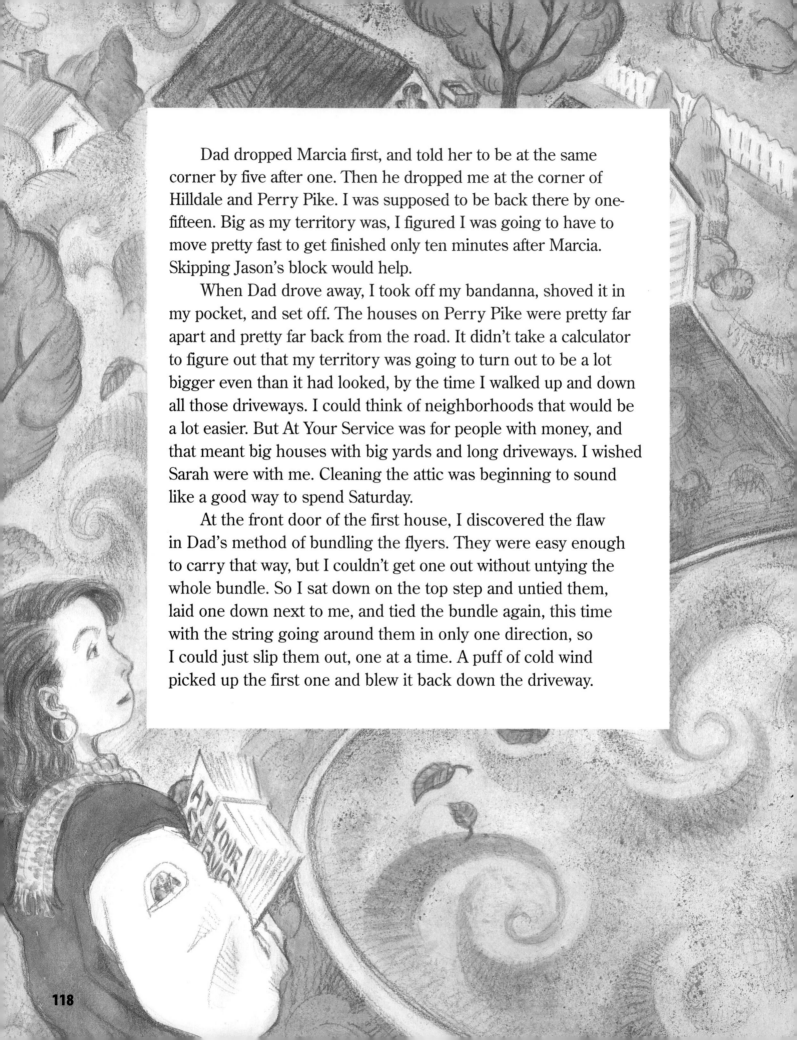

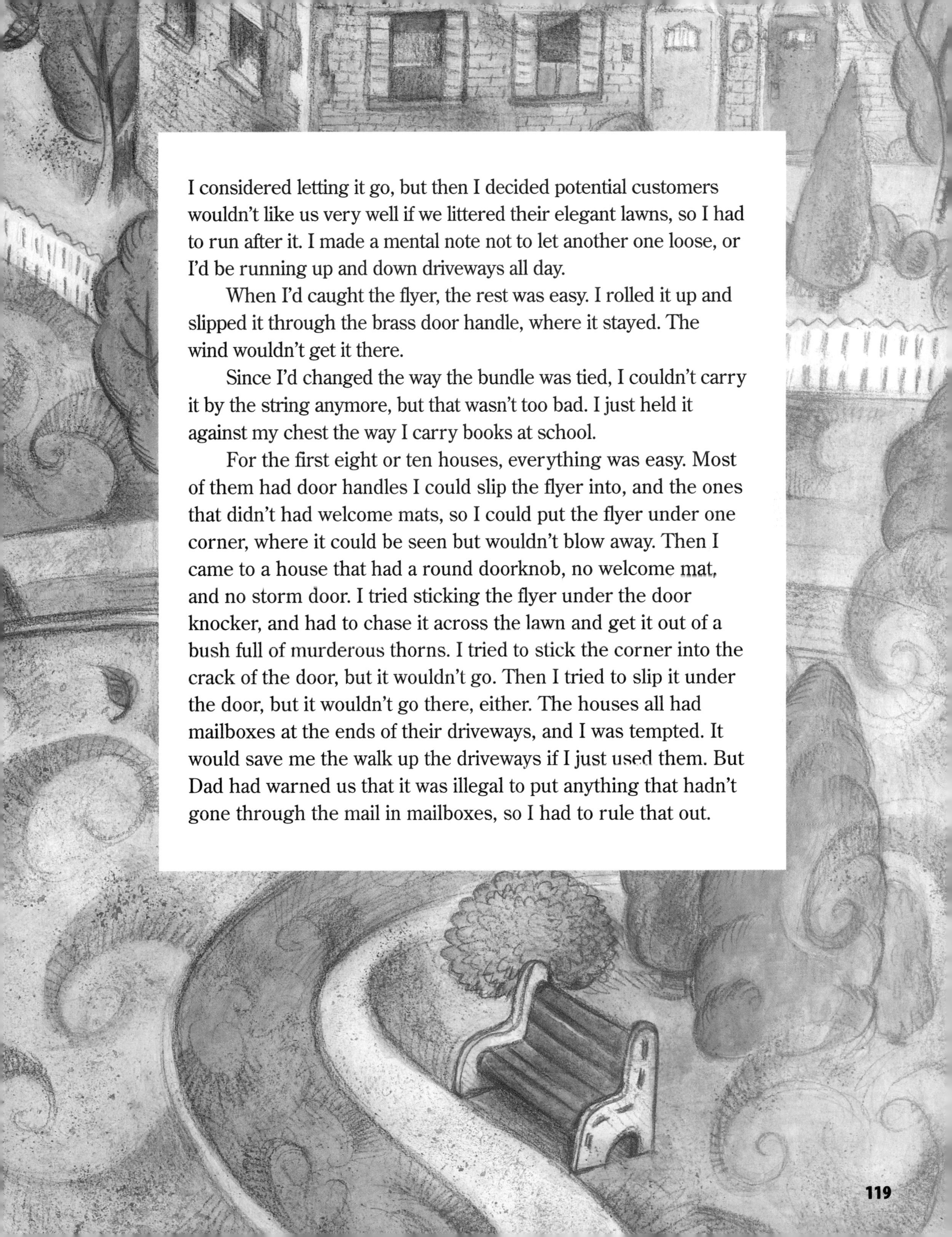

I considered letting it go, but then I decided potential customers wouldn't like us very well if we littered their elegant lawns, so I had to run after it. I made a mental note not to let another one loose, or I'd be running up and down driveways all day.

When I'd caught the flyer, the rest was easy. I rolled it up and slipped it through the brass door handle, where it stayed. The wind wouldn't get it there.

Since I'd changed the way the bundle was tied, I couldn't carry it by the string anymore, but that wasn't too bad. I just held it against my chest the way I carry books at school.

For the first eight or ten houses, everything was easy. Most of them had door handles I could slip the flyer into, and the ones that didn't had welcome mats, so I could put the flyer under one corner, where it could be seen but wouldn't blow away. Then I came to a house that had a round doorknob, no welcome mat, and no storm door. I tried sticking the flyer under the door knocker, and had to chase it across the lawn and get it out of a bush full of murderous thorns. I tried to stick the corner into the crack of the door, but it wouldn't go. Then I tried to slip it under the door, but it wouldn't go there, either. The houses all had mailboxes at the ends of their driveways, and I was tempted. It would save me the walk up the driveways if I just used them. But Dad had warned us that it was illegal to put anything that hadn't gone through the mail in mailboxes, so I had to rule that out.

Finally, I pried up one corner of a flagstone and put the flyer underneath so most of it stuck out. I hoped nobody had seen me prying up the stone. It made me feel like a vandal or something.

After that, I didn't have too much trouble figuring out places to put the flyers. I just got colder—my ears felt as if they were going to fall off by the time I'd been out an hour—and my hands got red and stiff. I figured Ben's hands were probably frozen to his handlebars. And I got tireder. Maybe Marcia's territory was hillier than mine, but I couldn't believe it. I'd start a street, thinking it was just a little hill, and by the time I was halfway up the block, it would start to feel like an assault on Everest.

A couple of times I met people coming out of their houses, and I handed the flyers right to them. I don't know what I expected that to be like—scary and awful, or something—but it wasn't bad at all. Everybody was very nice, and one guy glanced at the flyer and said he thought it was the best idea he'd ever heard. He said he already had about ten things he could think of for At Your Service to do, and he could probably come up with about ten more if he stopped to think about it. He wanted to know if we washed and waxed cars—when I came up the driveway, he'd been getting into a really gorgeous silver sports car—and I said I thought we'd be glad to. A car that size couldn't be too bad, and it was the kind of job Ben could probably do. I began to think maybe the Skinners could be in the 30 percent after all.

At one house a lady came to the door just as I was putting the flyer in her door handle. She read it, said she might have some business for us (I could hear at least two little dogs yipping and yapping in the background), and then said I looked cold. I said it was pretty chilly out, and she brought me a hot chocolate in a Styrofoam cup. “If nothing else, it'll help warm your hands.”

So I was feeling pretty good when everything went to pieces. I'd stopped to check my map to be sure I could skip Jason Felton's block, and I laid down my bundle of flyers. They were still tied, but I'd given out so many that the string was pretty loose. The wind caught them and scattered about half the rest. It took me nearly fifteen minutes to round them all up. That was bad enough. But then, because my ears were absolutely freezing, I decided to put the bandanna back on. After all, I hadn't seen anybody I knew, and I was skipping Jason's block, so it didn't seem to matter if I looked like a geek or not. How was I to know that the very next house on my route was David Wilson's house? And how was I to know that David Wilson had had Jason Felton spend the night at his house? And how was I to know that in spite of the terrible weather, they were outside playing basketball by David's garage, which happened to be, of course, at the end of the driveway I was walking up? By the time I saw them and saw who it was, they'd seen me and seen who I was.

If I'd been able to disappear, even if it meant going straight down into the ground and never being seen again, I think I'd have done it. I wanted to turn around and run back down the driveway, which I couldn't do, of course, because that would have been even less cool than wearing a bandanna and handing out flyers for the business one's family has gone into because one's father's been fired! The only thing I did was to snatch the bandanna off my head, and smile in what I hoped was a normal, casual way.

“Hi, guys!” I said. “I didn't expect to see you here.”

“Why not?” David said. “I live here.”

“She means me, you jerk,” Jason said.

No, I thought, Jason is definitely not classy. But I kept my smile in place as well as I could. “Would you like to give one of these flyers to your folks?” I asked David, and held one out.

He took it. “They're not home.”

“There's no rush. You can just leave it where they'll see it.”

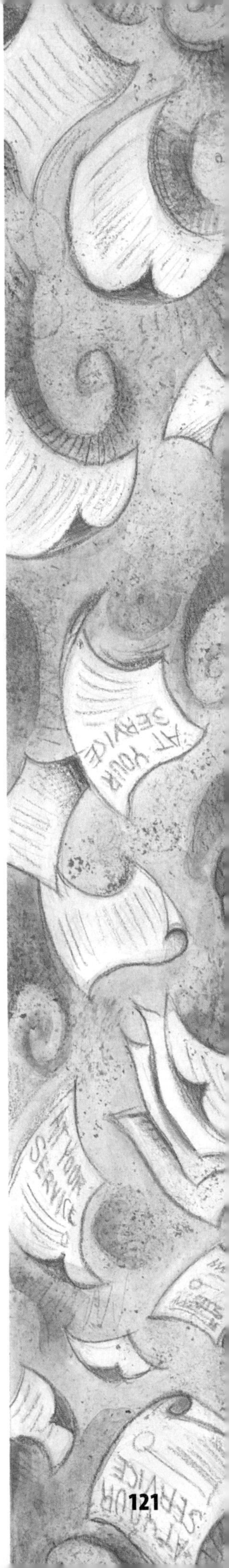

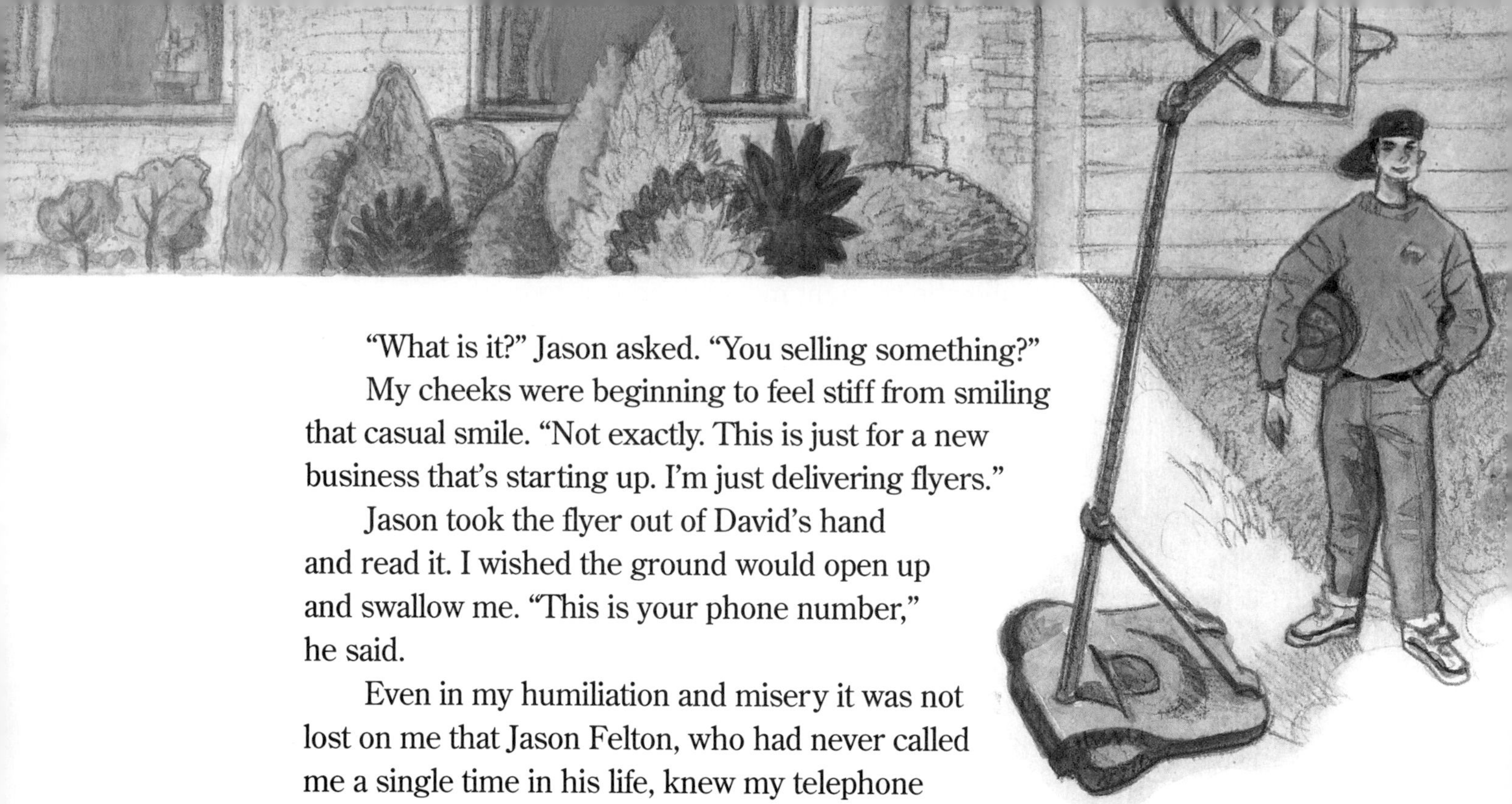

"What is it?" Jason asked. "You selling something?"

My cheeks were beginning to feel stiff from smiling that casual smile. "Not exactly. This is just for a new business that's starting up. I'm just delivering flyers."

Jason took the flyer out of David's hand and read it. I wished the ground would open up and swallow me. "This is your phone number," he said.

Even in my humiliation and misery it was not lost on me that Jason Felton, who had never called me a single time in his life, knew my telephone number by heart. Maybe he had some class, after all. "Right," I said, and the smile wasn't quite as hard to maintain. "It's my dad's business."

Jason grinned. He definitely had the most adorable grin I'd ever seen. "You going to work for him?"

"Sometimes, I guess. When I feel like it."

In spite of the cold, I could feel my cheeks and ears getting hot. I hoped the blush wouldn't show too much. "I've got to get going," I said. "I've got a lot of territory to cover."

"Okay," Jason said. "See you Monday." He handed the flyer back to David, and I turned back toward the street.

"We'll be calling, won't we, Jase? I can think of all sorts of 'services' I need. We'll be calling!" David shouted after me, as I hurried back down the driveway. I hated David Wilson. Loathed and despised David Wilson. And until the rain started, I fantasized horrible tortures for David Wilson.

But when the rain started, I knew that the only thing I had to wish for David Wilson was that he'd have to deliver flyers in the rain without a hat or gloves or an umbrella. The first few drops weren't

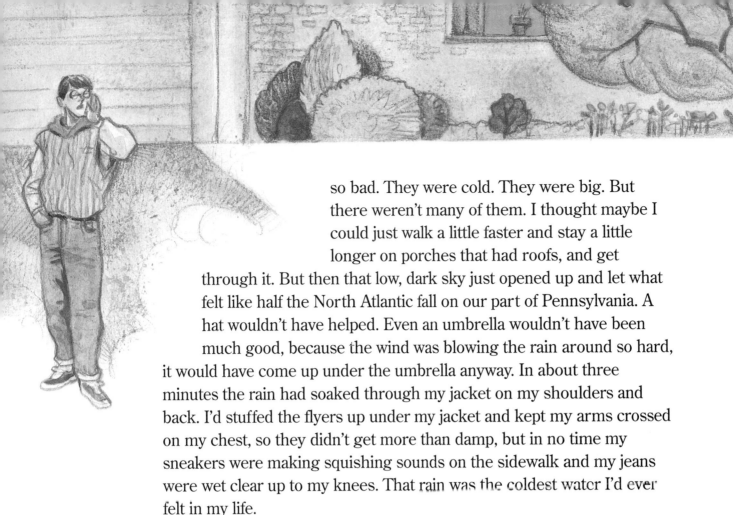

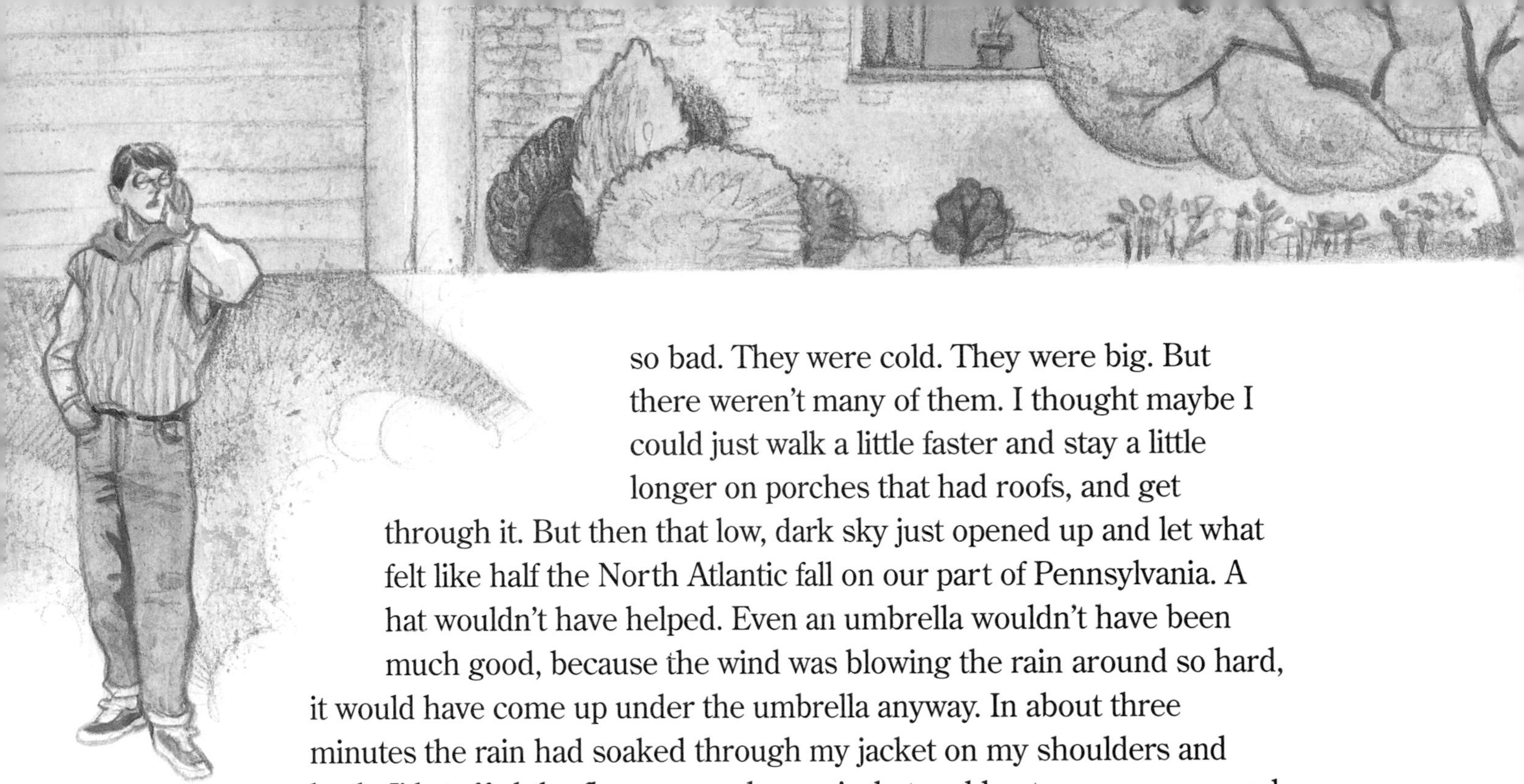

so bad. They were cold. They were big. But there weren't many of them. I thought maybe I could just walk a little faster and stay a little longer on porches that had roofs, and get through it. But then that low, dark sky just opened up and let what felt like half the North Atlantic fall on our part of Pennsylvania. A hat wouldn't have helped. Even an umbrella wouldn't have been much good, because the wind was blowing the rain around so hard, it would have come up under the umbrella anyway. In about three minutes the rain had soaked through my jacket on my shoulders and back. I'd stuffed the flyers up under my jacket and kept my arms crossed on my chest, so they didn't get more than damp, but in no time my sneakers were making squishing sounds on the sidewalk and my jeans were wet clear up to my knees. That rain was the coldest water I'd ever felt in my life.

It was only noon. I still had an hour and fifteen minutes, and nearly a third of my route to go. It wouldn't even do me any good to go back to my corner, I decided, because Dad wouldn't be there until one-fifteen. So I just kept going, hoping that eventually I'd get numb and not feel anything anymore. Hoping someone else would offer me a cup of hot chocolate. Finally, as I came out from under the trees at the end of a particularly long driveway, rain dripping off my nose and running down my bangs and into my eyes, I heard a horn honking, and there was the van. Marcia, looking as wet and miserable as I felt, was in the front seat, and Ben and his bicycle were in the back.

"Boy, am I glad to see you," I said, when I got in.

"Why didn't you go back to your corner when it started to rain?" Dad asked. "We've had to go up and down every street in your territory trying to find you! We didn't even know which way you'd gone first."

"But you said you'd pick me up at one-fifteen. I didn't see any sense in going back there and waiting in the rain. I figured I might as well deliver the rest of my flyers."

"Use your head, Jenny. You really didn't think I was going to leave you out in this."

"I didn't know."

"Well, next time you will. Marcia went straight back to her corner."

"I got just as wet as Jenny, though," Marcia pointed out.

"Yes, but you weren't out there so long because it was easy to find you," Dad said. Then he turned around and smiled at me. "Sorry, Jenny. It was very loyal of you to keep working. I shouldn't grump at you. How'd it go? Except for the rain, I mean."

"Okay, I guess." Except for David Wilson, I thought. "The people I got to talk to really seemed to like the idea."

"Good. Great! Now let's go home and get into dry clothes and have lunch. We can compare notes when we've warmed up." He pulled away, and I took my pack of damp flyers out from under my jacket. I was surprised to see how many I'd handed out. My bundle was nearly gone.

Ben was scowling. "The people I talked to liked the idea, too. If Dad hadn't made me get in the van, I could have made a fortune this afternoon! The rain made it better."

I shivered. "Better? How?"

"I was doing cars in a grocery store parking lot and people wanted me to start working right away. They thought one of the services should be carrying their groceries out to their cars. They tipped me for it. At first only a couple of people asked me to help. But when the rain started, business went bananas. People wanted to run out and get into their cars and let me do the rest." He dug into his pocket and held out a bundle of dollar bills. "Nobody gave me less than a dollar. One guy didn't have any

singles, and he gave me a whole five! I'd barely gotten started when Dad made me quit. The store was jammed. I could've been rich!"

"And you could've gotten flyers to a lot more places if you hadn't started carrying groceries in the first place," Dad said. "At Your Service doesn't even start until a week from Monday. The mission today was preliminary advertising, that's all."

"But it's *money*," Ben said.

"The first job is to get the word out. The money comes later. We've still got some legal matters to take care of before we get started."

"Does that mean I can keep everything I made today?"

Dad sighed as he turned into our driveway. "Okay. But tomorrow, if the weather's all right, you're handing out the rest of your flyers."

Before Ben had a chance to react, Mom, a raincoat draped over her head and shoulders, pounded on Dad's door. He opened it. "Have you got Rick with you?" she asked.

"No. Isn't he home? He should have been back by eleven."

"Well, he wasn't. He isn't. I don't know where he is."

"Okay, okay, Ellie, don't panic. Marcia and Ben, you go inside. Jenny, you come up in the front seat and we'll go look for him. He's got to be somewhere in the neighborhood."

"Fifteen minutes," Mom said. "If you aren't back in fifteen minutes, I'm calling the police."

"Take it easy," Dad said. "He's just gone inside somewhere to get out of the rain."

"Or been kidnapped. All that talk about strangers!"

"Go in. We'll be back in no time." Dad shut the door, and I moved up to the front seat. The others ran through the puddles, back toward the house. I wasn't worried.

"Go over to Pete's," I told Dad. "I guarantee you he'll be there."

"That's not part of his territory," Dad said.

"I know it. But it's only a block over. I'll make you a bet."

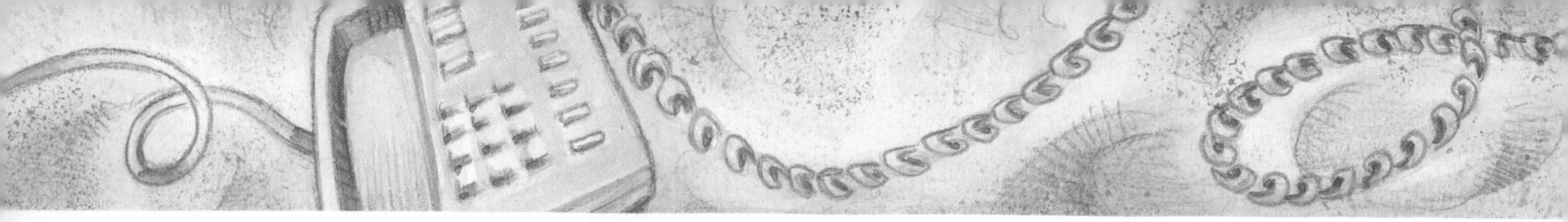

As we drove, we could tell Rick had been around the neighborhood. Soggy flyers were on driveways, in the gutters, on people's lawns. And the path led directly from our next-door neighbors' to Pete's house. Rick, in his stocking feet, with a chocolate chip cookie in his hand, came to the door when Pete's mother called him, all innocence. "It isn't one-thirty yet," he said, looking at Mom's watch. "Do I really have to come now?"

I nodded. "If you want to live through the rest of the day, you'd better come now." He came.

Just as I'd thought, he hadn't been listening when Dad explained the job. He'd understood about his territory and everything—and he'd covered it completely. Exactly as he was supposed to, except that he also did the block Pete's house was on because he wanted to go to Pete's. The trouble was, he hadn't heard what Dad had said about where to put the flyers. He'd just put one down in front of every door. And almost as soon as he'd put them down, the wind had taken them away. I don't think he even noticed. He was really surprised that Dad was so mad. Really surprised that he hadn't done everything just right. By the time we got home, Rick was in tears. I was having trouble blinking back tears myself, and Mom burst out crying the moment she saw him, she was so relieved. Then she got mad and chewed him out all the way to the kitchen.

Hot chocolate helped a little, but it wasn't exactly a happy group that gathered in the kitchen a little later. Mom said she would have thought of calling Pete's house to see if Rick had gone there, except that the phone had been ringing all morning. The flyer hadn't mentioned that At Your Service wouldn't actually go into operation for another week, and people had wanted us to start immediately. Some people had been understanding, Mom said, and just asked when they should call back. But others had been nasty. One man had accused her of false advertising and threatened to call the Better Business Bureau. A woman wanted a party catered on Friday night and got very upset when Mom said we didn't do catering.

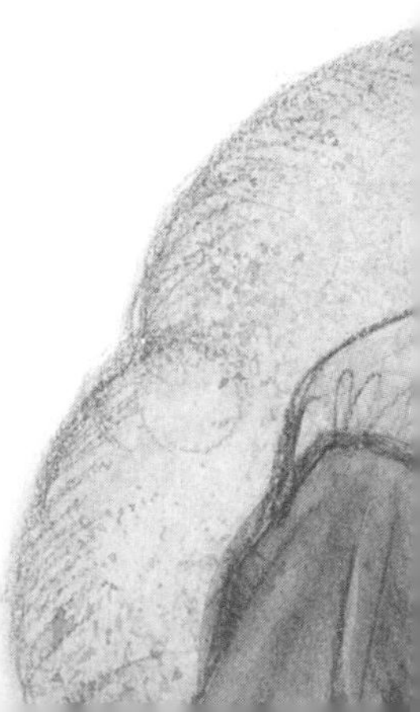

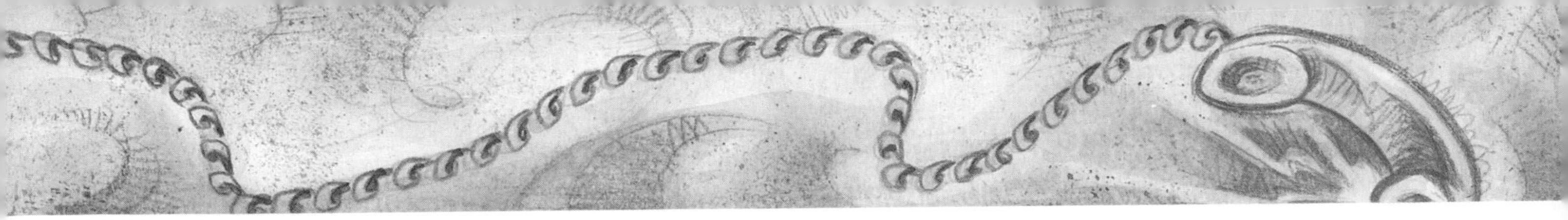

She said the flyer had distinctly said "We do it all." The woman had not agreed that figurative speaking was appropriate in an advertising flyer. Mom had found her a caterer in the Yellow Pages, and she'd taken the number. But she'd hung up without saying good-bye.

Mom hadn't even realized how late it was, or even that it was raining, until after noon, and it was then that she'd started to get worried about Rick. But the phone kept ringing, so she hadn't really had time to think clearly. Finally, she'd taken the phone off the hook and we'd gotten home only a few minutes later.

The phone was still off the hook. "Maybe we shouldn't have done this on a Saturday," Mom said. "People all seem to be finding their flyers right away."

"Except mine," Rick said, sounding about to cry again. "Mine are all blown away. Nobody'll ever be able to read mine! I'm a failure. I always do everything wrong!"

Dad had forgiven Rick by this time. "Never mind, Rick. You can always take some others around later." He leaned back in his chair and blew on his hot chocolate. "I can't believe it," he said. "Calls already. People wanting us to begin now. It's beyond my wildest dreams."

"Mine, too," Mom said. "Mine, too." I didn't think she meant it exactly the way Dad did.

"This is it, Ellie," Dad said, grinning his chief-executive-officer grin. "We're off! And we're going to be part of the thirty percent. You'll see! We're going to make it!"

SOURCE

U.S. Department of Labor

THE SERVICE INDUSTRY

In *The Great Skinner Enterprise,* Jenny's father enlists the help of his family to start a personal service business. Personal services, such as running errands, are just a tiny part of what's called the "service sector." As the name implies, the service industry provides services — such as education, health care, and recreation — rather than agricultural products (such as corn) or manufactured goods (such as skateboards or CDs). Waiters, nurses, and teachers are just a few examples of service workers.

The Skinners aren't the only ones who are adapting to the changing American business scene by finding service jobs. This booming sector is the fastest growing part of the American economy, as these charts make clear.

GROWTH OF SERVICE JOBS, 1900–1990

The percentage of Americans with service jobs has climbed steadily since 1900.

	1900	1930	1960	1990
Agriculture	44%	21%	6%	3%
Industry	36%	40%	40%	26%
Service	20%	39%	54%	71%

Source: U.S. Department of Labor

FUTURE GROWTH OF SERVICE JOBS

Experts believe that jobs will keep shifting from goods-producing industries to the service sector. By 2005, the service sector will account for four out of every five jobs.

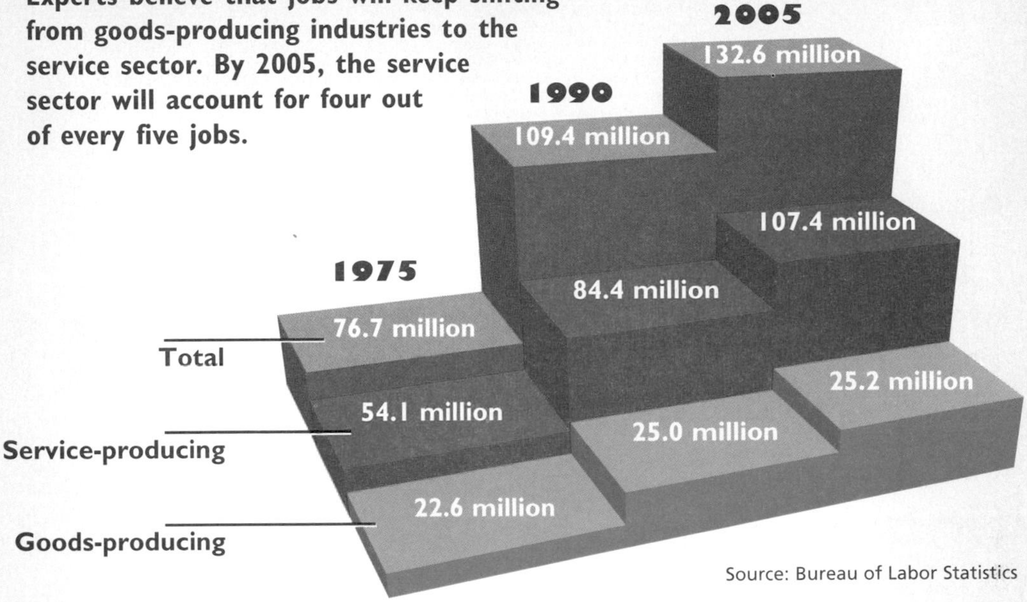

Source: Bureau of Labor Statistics

FAST GROWING FIELDS

The service industry has plenty of career opportunities. The health care field will need the most new employees (13 million), while social services will have the fastest growth — 59 percent.

Employment in Service Industries, 1990 and Projected 2005 (millions)

Industry	Employment 1990	Employment 2005	Change, 1990–2005 Number[1]	Change, 1990–2005 Percent
Total	37.5	50.5	13.0	35
Health, public and private	8.9	12.8	3.9	44
Business services	5.2	7.6	2.4	45
Education, public and private	9.4	11.8	2.3	25
Engineering and management	2.5	3.8	1.3	52
Social services	1.8	2.9	1.1	59
Hotels	1.6	2.2	.5	32
Legal services	.9	1.4	.5	55
Amusement and recreation	1.1	1.4	.3	31
Auto repair and related services	.9	1.2	.3	34
Personal services	1.1	1.3	.2	20

Source: Bureau of Labor Statistics

[1]Figures for 1990 employment plus change may not sum to projected 2005 employment due to rounding.

PROJECT

How to

Create a Business Plan

Starting a business takes *planning*—and plenty of it.

It takes a lot of planning to start a business and keep it running. Most entrepreneurs create business plans to keep track of important details. A business plan includes information about the product a business sells or the service it provides; plans for production, advertising, and distribution; details about how the business will make and spend money; and information about how it will attract customers and compete with other businesses.

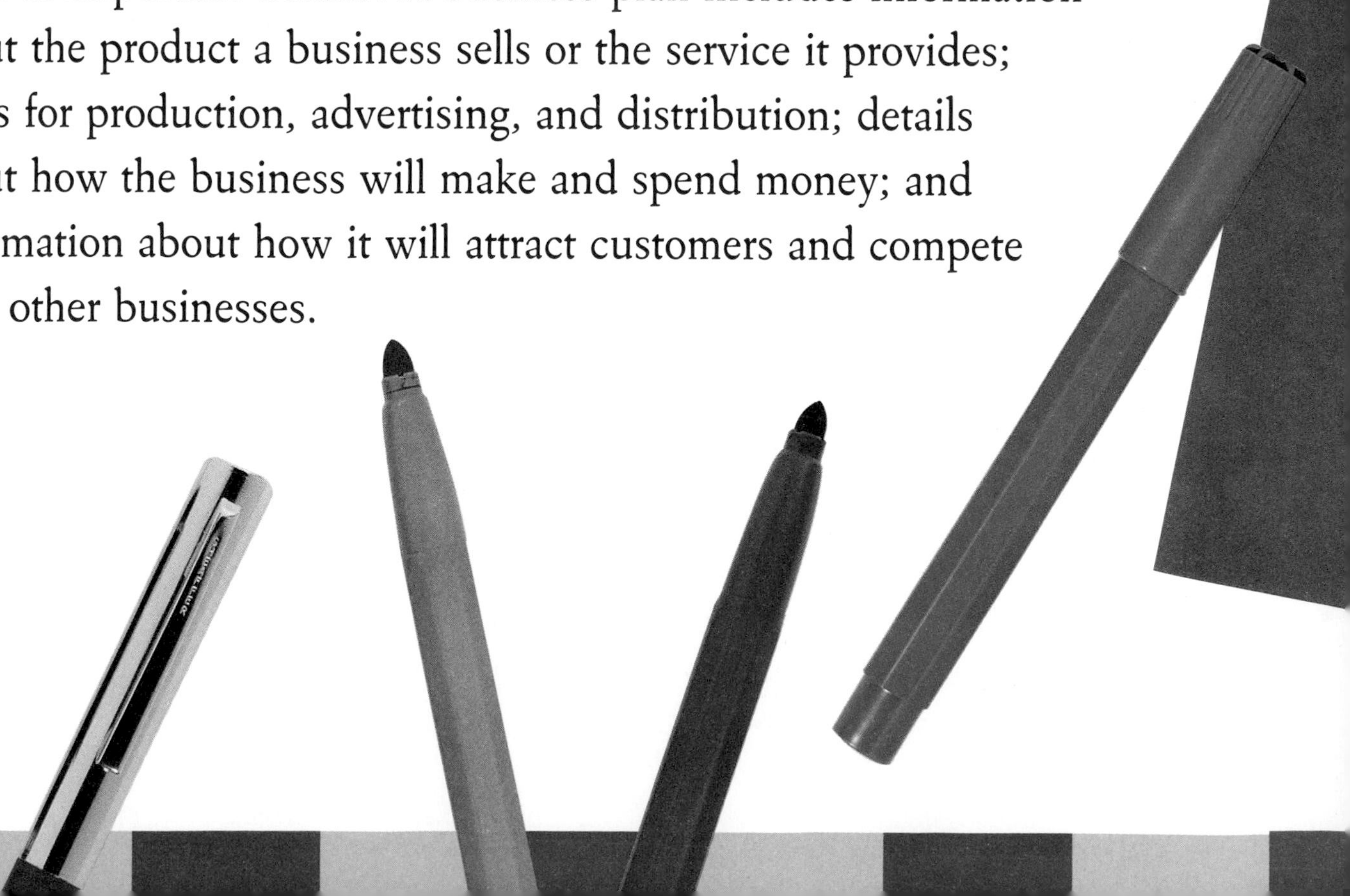

Business Plan
Terrific T-shirts, Inc.
T
Market Research
Materials
Advertising Budget

1 Research and Organize Your Business

What kind of business is right for you and your team? Brainstorm and research ideas for a business you could start together. Look at books to find out how different types of businesses are run. If possible, interview a local businessperson. Write down your ideas, and decide as a group which idea you like best. (If you've already done a feasibility study, you may want to use the idea you came up with.)

TOOLS

- notebook and pencil
- paper and markers
- pocket calculator
- folder

Think about possible customers. Are there enough to support your business? Analyze your competition. Are other companies providing the same product or service? Are they doing a good job?

How many people will you need to run your business? What will each person need to do? Write a job description for each position. If you learned how to make an organizational chart in Workshop 2, you might want to make one now.

2 Chart Your Course

Plan what your company will offer. If your business will be manufacturing a product:

- make a diagram or drawing of your product and describe it in detail.
- figure out where to manufacture your product.
- decide how to distribute your product to your customers.

If your business will be providing a service:

- describe your service.
- figure out how many people will be needed to provide the service.
- look at a map and decide where your headquarters should be.

Before you go on, take a minute to answer these questions with your group:

- Did we choose a business with a good chance of succeeding?
- Will our business have a job for everyone in the group?
- Can we describe our product or service in detail?

3 Make a Budget and an Advertising Plan

How much money will you need to start your business? Add up all the expenses you will have. How much will materials cost? What will you spend on advertising? Will you have to pay salaries or labor costs? Estimate as accurately as possible how much it will cost to make your product or provide your service. Finally, figure out how much money you expect to make in sales. Will your company make more money than it costs to run? In other words, will your business make a profit?

Make a list of all of the different ways you could advertise your product or service. What is the best way to reach your customers? Do they read the newspaper? listen to the radio? read flyers? Decide how you want to spend the advertising money in your budget, and include a sample advertisement in your plan.

Tip **Think about what kind of advertisements catch your eye. Look at newspaper ads and flyers to help you come up with design ideas.**

4 Put It All Together

Use all the information you've gathered to draft your business plan. Be sure your plan covers each area your team investigated: preliminary research, organization, description of product or service, budget, and advertising.

Next, choose a company name and a logo. Put all the pieces together in a folder to create your business-plan portfolio. Be sure to include all of your research, charts, and drawings.

If You Are Using a Computer . . .

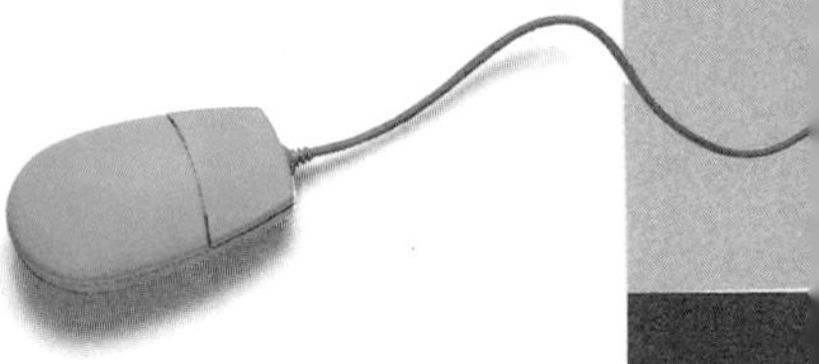

Use the computer to draft your business plan. If you have a spreadsheet program, you can use it to make the budget. Then include the budget and a description of your product or service in a brochure that you create on the computer.

CONGRATULATIONS

Now you know what it takes to plan a successful business. You can use this information to start a business of your own someday!

Ben and Jerry
Entrepreneurs

Glossary

ad cam•paign
(ad kam pān′) *noun*
A series of marketing operations designed to generate public awareness and sales of a product or service. The owner of the jeans company hoped the new *ad campaign* would increase sales.

a•gen•cy
(ā′ jən sē) *noun*
An organization or company that is authorized to do business for other groups or individuals.

aus•ter•i•ty
(ô ster′i tē) *noun*
An extremely simple or frugal way of life without comforts or luxuries.

cap•i•tal (kap′ i tl) *noun*
The money needed to start up a business. With *capital* borrowed from the bank, I started my own business.

capital

com•pe•ti•tion
(kom′ pi tish′ ən) *noun*
The rivalry offered by another business. I wanted to open my own ice-cream shop, but the *competition* looked too stiff.

co-op (kō′ op) *noun*
A group whose members produce goods and sell them to share the profits.

e•con•o•my
(i kon′ ə mē) *noun*
The management of the resources of a community or country.

en•ter•prise
(en′ tər prīz′) *noun*
Any business, especially one that is important or takes a lot of energy.

en•tre•pre•neurs
(än′ trə prə nûrz′) *noun*
People who start up and manage a business usually at some risk.
▲ **entrepreneur**

es•ti•mate
(es′ tə mit) *noun*
A general but careful guess at the cost, size, or value of something.

fo•cus groups
(fō′ kəs grōōps) *noun*
Groups of experts who gather to discuss a product, topic, or problem.
▲ **focus group**

hired hands
(hīrd handz) *noun*
People employed by a farm owner to help with the farm work.
▲ **hired hand**

in•cor•po•rated
(in kôr′ pə rā′ tid) *verb*
Formed into a corporation. Before opening his store to the public, the owner *incorporated* his business.
▲ **incorporate**

in•vest•ments
(in vest′ mənts) *noun*
The using or lending of money for a business in order to get a profit in return. ▲ **investment**

in•voic•es
(in′ vois əz) *noun*
Detailed lists of goods shipped for services rendered, with an account of all costs; bills.
▲ **invoice**

manufactured goods

line (līn) *noun*
The types of goods that a company sells. Our product *line* includes toys, games, and stuffed animals.

live•stock
(līv′ stok′) *noun*
The horses, cattle, sheep, and other profitable animals kept on a farm or ranch.

man•u•fac•tured goods
(man′ yə fak′chərd go͝odz) *noun*
Products that are made by people, especially in a factory, rather than grown or harvested from nature.

mar•ket re•search
(mär′ kit ri sûrch′) *noun*
A study undertaken to see what buyers want, need, or think about a particular product.

a	add	o͝o	took	ə =
ā	ace	o͞o	pool	a in *above*
â	care	u	up	e in *sicken*
ä	palm	û	burn	i in *possible*
e	end	yo͞o	fuse	o in *melon*
ē	equal	oi	oil	u in *circus*
i	it	ou	pout	
ī	ice	ng	ring	
o	odd	th	thin	
ō	open	t͟h	this	
ô	order	zh	vision	

Glossary

mar•ket•ing cam•paign
(mär′ ki ting kam pān′)
noun
A plan to locate potential buyers of a product or service, and to convince them of its advantages over similar products or services.

mer•chan•dis•ers
(mûr′ chən dīz′ərz) *noun*
People who buy and sell goods for profit.
▲ **merchandiser**

Word History

Merchandiser is a form of the word *merchant*, which comes from the Latin word *mercari*, which means "to trade" or "to buy."

part•ners
(pärt′ nərz) *noun*
Two or more people who invest money in a business and share its profits and risks. ▲ **partner**

pastureland

shelf presence

pas•ture•land
(pas′ chər land′) *noun*
Farmland that is used for grazing cattle, sheep, or other animals. We use one of our fields for planting corn and the other for *pastureland.*

press re•leas•es
(pres′ rē lēs′ əz) *noun*
Brief written statements sent out by individuals and organizations to newspapers and other media, to describe, explain, or publicize events. The company sent out several *press releases* to advertise the opening of its new store. ▲ **press release**

prod•uct man•ag•er
(prod′ əkt man′ i jər)
noun
The person in charge of promoting a company's goods; the job includes market research and advertising.

pro•spec•tive
(prə spek′ tiv) *adjective*
Possible or expected; future.

re•tail•ing
(rē′ tā ling) *verb*
Selling goods to consumers. In our store, we are *retailing* shirts and ties. ▲ **retail**

sales pro•jec•tion
(sālz prə jek′ shən) *noun*
A prediction of what will sell.

sam•pling
(sam′ pling) *noun*
The part of a whole that has been tested.

sec•tor (sek′ tər) *noun*
A certain part of a group or industry.

Word History

Sector comes from the Latin word *sectus*, which means "to cut."

serv•ice in•dus•try
(sûr′ vis in′ də strē) *noun*
Businesses whose members perform work for others.

shel pres•ence
(shelf prez′ əns) *noun*
The way a product appears on the shelf in a store; the degree to which a product on a shelf will attract consumers' interest.

spokes•per•son
(spōks′ pûr′ sən) *noun*
Someone who speaks on behalf of a business or organization.

stock cer•tif•i•cates
(stok sər tif′ i kits) *noun*
Documents issued by a business to a stockholder, to show how many shares of stock he or she owns.
▲ **stock certificate**

stock•hold•ers
(stok′ hōl′ dərz) *noun*
People who hold stock in a corporation.
▲ **stockholder**

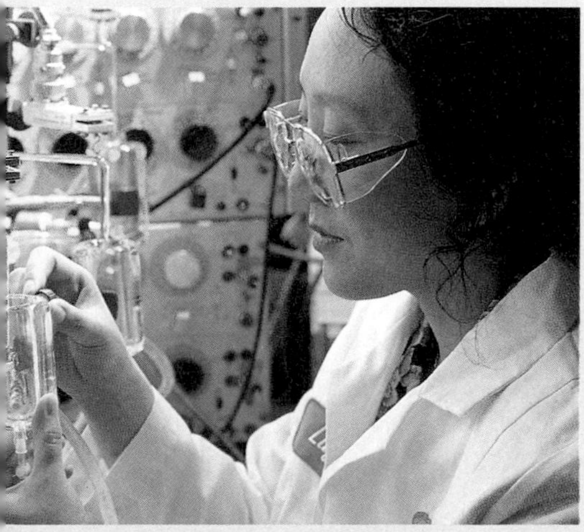

technician

sur•vey (sər vā′) *verb*
To collect data from people about a specific topic or idea, usually by asking a series of questions.

Word Study

Survey can also be used as a noun, referring to the list of questions used in the study.

tech•ni•cian
(tek nish′ ən) *noun*
A person who is skilled in a particular job, especially someone who has been trained to handle special equipment or perform special procedures. The medical *technician* ran several tests on the patient.

till (til) *verb*
To work the land in preparation for raising crops, as by plowing and fertilizing.

tract (trakt) *noun*
A large stretch of land.

trade•mark
(trād′ märk′) *noun*
A symbol that appears on a product for the purpose of distinguishing it from products sold by competitors.

trademark

till

a add	o͝o took	ə =
ā ace	o͞o pool	a in *above*
â care	u up	e in *sicken*
ä palm	û burn	i in *possible*
e end	yo͞o fuse	o in *melon*
ē equal	oi oil	u in *circus*
i it	ou pout	
ī ice	ng ring	
o odd	th thin	
ō open	*th* this	
ô order	zh vision	

Authors & Illustrators

George Ancona *pages 92–105*

This award-winning photographer has worked on more than 40 books and a number of films. Each project has allowed him to travel to new places and meet new people. He says, "Photographing, filming, or writing . . . about someone or something is my way of feeling alive and in touch with the world around me. I believe that work does this for many people."

Tony Caldwell *pages 10–25*

Tony Caldwell's illustrations are lively and fun. This artist has a unique approach to drawing. When he does the preliminary sketches for a new work, such as *The Toothpaste Millionaire,* he often gets so involved that he acts out the story as he draws it.

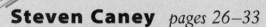

Steven Caney *pages 26–33*

Steven Caney likes sharing his bright ideas with people. He has written books on inventions, contraptions, games, and toys. Besides being a writer, Steven Caney is a successful toy and game inventor. This author really tries hard to spark kids' imaginations.

Jean Merrill *pages 10–25*

Jean Merrill grew up on a farm on Lake Ontario in New York State. That meant that she was able to spend a lot of time swimming, tobogganing, and playing outdoors when school wasn't in session. "The only thing that could keep me indoors was a book—but a book could also be carried up into a tree, out to a meadow, down by the lakeside," she says. The fact that she was able to explore, invent, build, daydream, and discover may have had a great deal to do with her eventual choice of writing as a profession.

Phyllis Reynolds Naylor *pages 54–65*

Phyllis Reynolds Naylor isn't happy unless she spends some time writing each day. She has written over 75 books for children, young adults, and adults. She admits that almost everything that happens to her, her two sons, and other people she knows ends up in one of her books—all mixed up, of course, with imaginings.

Stephanie Tolan *pages 112–127*

From the time she was nine years old, Stephanie Tolan knew that she would become a writer. As a child, she loved to read and would stay up as late as she could—just to finish another chapter in a favorite book. At first she wrote poetry and plays, but working with schoolchildren as part of the Poets-in-the-Schools project inspired her to begin her first novel. Now she says she writes not only for herself but also for the kids she hopes will find her stories "worth staying up late to finish."

Books &

Author Study

More by Phyllis Reynolds Naylor

To Walk the Sky Path
Billie Tomie is proud of his Seminole heritage, but he also likes spending time with Jeff Miller and other kids in school who live their lives according to other traditions. Billy must decide which path to follow if he's to be true to himself.

How I Came to Be a Writer
Naylor talks about what inspired her to be a writer, from her first work in kindergarten to her most recent books.

The Agony of Alice
A young girl records the ups and downs of being a teenager in her journal, which she has named "The Agony of Alice."

Fiction

Good-Bye, My Wishing Star
by Vicki Grove
A girl and her family find their lives are changed forever when they fall upon hard times and lose their farm.

Kid Power
by Susan Beth Pfeffer
Summer is a carefree time for most kids, but Janey wants to earn some spending money. She comes up with a great idea. She opens an employment agency just for kids.

Not for a Billion Gazillion Dollars
by Paula Danziger
Matthew Martin owes everyone money, so how can he possibly buy the computer program of his dreams? After a few unsuccessful business ventures, Matthew and his friend Jil! come up with a winner.

Nonfiction

Better Than a Lemonade Stand: Small Business Ideas for Kids
by Daryl Bernstein
If you are thinking about opening a business, here are some ideas to get you started.

Close Calls: From the Brink of Ruin to Business Success
by Nathan Aaseng
Every business faces problems. Here are the stories of some companies that were able to think creatively and become successful despite serious setbacks.

Sugaring Time
by Katherine Lasky
photographs by Christopher Knight
Where does the syrup for your pancakes come from? Learn how a Vermont family works together to gather maple syrup in the fall.

xMedia

Videos

Famous Amos: The Business Behind the Cookie
(Coronet)
Meet Wally Amos, and learn how he built a cookie empire out of an old family recipe. (30 minutes)

Math... Who Needs It?
(FASE Productions)
This PBS special features Jaime Escalante and his students from East Los Angeles. Join them, and comedian Paul Rodriguez, as they visit various professionals and talk about how they use math in their jobs. (52 minutes)

You Must Remember This
(WonderWorks)
What was it like to make movies in the 1940s? Ella finds out when she discovers that her great uncle was one of the most respected African-American film directors of that era. (60 minutes)

Software

Hot Dog Stand
Wings (IBM, Macintosh)
How much money can you make selling hot dogs at a football game? This program allows you to decide how much food to buy and helps you keep track of your expenses and figure out how to make a profit.

The Market Place
MECC (Apple, IBM)
Your friendly neighborhood lemonade stand becomes a place to learn business skills in this simulated enterprise.

SimFarm
Maxis/Creative Pursuits (IBM)
Work as a team to develop your family farm into a profitable and responsible business. In order to succeed you must increase production without harming the environment.

Magazines

DynaMath
Scholastic Inc.
DynaMath uses comic strips, puzzles, and games to help you sharpen your math skills and learn how to apply them in everyday life and in business.

Zillions: Consumer Reports for Kids
Consumers Union of the United States
This magazine helps you get the best buys for your money. It compares brands and reports on what young people think about the products they use.

A Place to Write

This organization offers students the opportunity to learn firsthand how a business works. For information on special materials and programs available to sixth graders, write to:

Junior Achievement, Inc.
1 Education Way
Colorado Springs, CO 80906

Acknowledgments

Grateful acknowledgment is made to the following sources for permission to reprint from previously published material. The publisher has made diligent efforts to trace the ownership of all copyrighted material in this volume and believes that all necessary permissions have been secured. If any errors or omissions have inadvertently been made, proper corrections will gladly be made in future editions.

Cover: Danny Pelavin.

Interior: Selection and cover from THE TOOTHPASTE MILLIONAIRE by Jean Merrill. Copyright © 1972 by Houghton Mifflin Company. Reprinted by permission of Houghton Mifflin Company. All rights reserved.

"Choosing a Business," "Making a Business Plan," and cover from STEVEN CANEY'S KIDS' AMERICA. Copyright © 1978 by Steven Caney. Used by permission of Workman Publishing Company, Inc. All rights reserved.

Selection and cover from BEN & JERRY: THE REAL SCOOP! by Jules Older, illustrated by Lyn Severance. Text copyright © 1993 by Jules Older. Illustrations copyright © 1993 by Lyn Severance. Published by Chapters Publishing Ltd., Shelburne, Vermont. Reprinted by permission of Publishers Development Group.

"Dog Walking Feasibility Study" adapted from "Best Ideas List," in FAST CASH FOR KIDS by Bonnie and Noel Drew. Copyright © 1990, 1991 by Bonnie and Noel Drew. Published by The Career Press. Reprinted by permission.

Selection and cover from EDDIE, INCORPORATED by Phyllis Reynolds Naylor, illustrated by Blanche Sims. Text copyright © 1980 by Phyllis Reynolds Naylor. Illustrations copyright © 1980 by Blanche Sims. Reprinted with the permission of Atheneum Books for Young Readers, Simon & Schuster Children's Publishing Division.

"Students Turn Greens Into Gold" by Molly O'Neill, June 15, 1994. Copyright © 1994 by the New York Times Company. Reprinted by permission.

"Food From the 'Hood" and the trademarked logo are used by permission of Food From the 'Hood, a natural food products company.

"The Jeans Team" by Nancy Fitzgerald. Text copyright © 1996 by Scholastic Inc.

"Levi's Gold" by Dorothy Slate from Cobblestone: The History Magazine for Young People, May 1989 issue: Entrepreneurs of the Past. Copyright © 1989 Cobblestone Publishing, Inc., 7 School Street, Peterborough, NH 03458. Reprinted by permission of the publisher.

Organizational Chart from TOM'S OF MAINE, INC. is used with their kind permission.

"The Adamses of Georgia" from THE AMERICAN FARM FAMILY by George Ancona and Joan Anderson. Photographs copyright © 1989 by George Ancona. Text copyright © 1989 by Joan Anderson. Reprinted by permission of Harcourt Brace & Company.

Selection and cover from HEARTLAND by Diane Siebert, illustrated by Wendell Minor. Text copyright © 1989 by Diane Siebert. Illustrations copyright © 1989 by Wendell Minor. Reprinted by permission of HarperCollins Publishers.

Selection from THE GREAT SKINNER ENTERPRISE by Stephanie S. Tolan. Copyright © 1986 by Stephanie S. Tolan. Reprinted with the permission of Simon & Schuster Books for Young Readers, an imprint of Simon & Schuster Children's Publishing Division. Cover from THE GREAT SKINNER ENTERPRISE by Stephanie S. Tolan. Copyright © 1988 by Viking Penguin, Inc. Used by permission of Puffin Books, a division of Penguin Books USA Inc.

Chart from Bulletin 2400-1, U.S. Department of Labor/Bureau of Labor Statistics.

Chart from Occupational Outlook Quarterly, Fall 1991. Published by U.S. Department of Labor/Bureau of Labor Statistics.

Cover from BONANZA GIRL by Patricia Beatty. Illustration copyright © 1993 by Toby Gowing. Published by William Morrow & Company, Inc.

Cover from FROM RAGS TO RICHES: PEOPLE WHO STARTED BUSINESSES FROM SCRATCH by Nathan Aaseng, illustrated by Stephen Clement. Illustration copyright © 1990 by Lerner Publications Company. Published by Lerner Publications Company.

Cover from THE STAR FISHER by Laurence Yep. Copyright © 1991 by William Morrow & Company, Inc. Published by William Morrow & Company, Inc.

Cover from THE TURTLE STREET TRADING CO. by Jill Ross Klevin, illustrated by Jacqueline Rogers. Illustration copyright © 1995 by Scholastic Inc. Originally published by Delacorte Press.

Photography and Illustration Credits

Selection Openers: Peter Spacek.

Photos: All Tools in Workshops and Project © John Lei for Scholastic Inc. unless otherwise noted. p. 2 tl: © John Bessler for Scholastic Inc.; bl: © John Lei for Scholastic Inc.; ml: © Stephen Ogilvy for Scholastic Inc. pp. 2-3 background: © Richard Nowitz. p. 3 bc: © Richard Nowitz; tc: © Dann Coffey/The Image Bank. p. 4 c: © Lillian Gee for Scholastic Inc.; tc: © Chris Mooney/FPG International Corp.; br: © David Lawrence for Scholastic Inc.; mr: © Paul O. Boisvert for Scholastic Inc. p. 5 c: © Lillian Gee for Scholastic Inc.; tc: © Chris Mooney/FPG International Corp. p. 6 c: © Lillian Gee for Scholastic Inc.; tc: © Chris Mooney/FPG International Corp. p. 26 c: © Stanley Bach for Scholastic Inc. p. 27: © Stanley Bach for Scholastic Inc. p. 28 bl: © Stanley Bach for Scholastic Inc.; tr: © Stephen Carr for Scholastic Inc. p. 29 bc: © David Waitz for Scholastic Inc. p. 33 br: © Ken Karp for Scholastic Inc. p. 44 ml: © Jay Blakesberg/Retna; tl, bl: © Paul O. Boisvert; tr: © David Lawrence for Scholastic Inc.; tc: © Dann Coffey/The Image Bank. pp. 44-45 c: © Paul O. Boisvert for Scholastic Inc. p. 45: © John Bessler for Scholastic Inc. p. 46 bl: © John Williams; mr: © Paul O. Boisvert; tr: © John Bessler for Scholastic Inc. p. 47 tc, bl: © John Bessler for Scholastic Inc.; mr: © Paul O. Boisvert for Scholastic Inc. p. 49 c: © David Lawrence for Scholastic Inc. p. 50 bc: Cover of book: © Lois & Bob Schlowsky/Tony Stone Images, book photo: © Lillian Gee for Scholastic Inc.; bl, ml: © Lillian Gee for Scholastic Inc. p. 51 bc: © Lillian Gee for Scholastic Inc.; br: © Paul O. Boisvert for Scholastic Inc. p. 67 tl: © Jim McHugh/Outline. p. T69 tr: © Jim McHugh/Outline. p. 70: © Nicole Katano for Scholastic Inc. p. 71 br: © Nicole Katano for Scholastic Inc.; bl: © Jim McHugh/Outline. p. 74 bc: © Comstock Inc. p. 75 tc: © Stephen Ogilvy for Scholastic Inc. p. 76 ml: © William Tautic/The Stock Market; tr: © Stephen Ogilvy for Scholastic Inc. p. 77 tr: © Fabricius & Taylor/Gamma Liaison. p. 78 tl: © R. Rappaport/Westlight; mr: © Ted Horowitz/The Stock Market. p. 79 tr: © Comstock Inc. p. 80 tr: © Stephen Ogilvy for Scholastic Inc.; tl: © Walter Hodges/Westlight; ml: © J.B. O'Rourke/The Stock Market. p. 81: © Stephen Ogilvy for Scholastic Inc. pp. 82-85: © Courtesy Levi Strauss & Co., San Francisco. p. 86 bl, tc: © David S. Waitz for Scholastic Inc.; mr: © Cole Riggs for Scholastic Inc. pp. 86-87 bc: © Lillian Gee for Scholastic Inc. p. 87 br: © Halley Ganges for Scholastic Inc.; tr: pencil: © Richard Lee for Scholastic Inc., fountain pens: © David Lawrence for Scholastic Inc. pp. 88-89 bc: © Lillian Gee for Scholastic Inc. p. 89 br: © Paul O. Boisvert for Scholastic Inc. p. 130 b: © David Lawrence for Scholastic Inc.; tc: © Lillian Gee for Scholastic Inc. p. 131 c: © Lillian Gee for Scholastic Inc. pp. 132-133: © Lillian Gee for Scholastic Inc. p. 134: © Lillian Gee for Scholastic Inc. p. 135 bc: © Lillian Gee for Scholastic Inc.; br: © Paul O. Boisvert for Scholastic Inc. p. 136 bc: © Bob O'Shaughnessy/The Stock Market. p. 137 tc: © Tom Carroll/Photobank, Inc. p. 138 tc: © Lillian Gee for Scholastic Inc.; bl: © Tony Craddock/Tony Stone Worldwide. p. 139 bl: © Terry Vine/Tony Stone Images; mr: © Tony Stone Images. p. 140 bl: © Courtesy of Tom Hinkie/Daily Tribune; ml: © Courtesy of Tony Caldwell; tl: © Courtesy of Penguin USA. p. 141 tr: © Courtesy McIntosh & Otis; br: © Courtesy of Stephanie Tolan. p. 143 br: © Stephen Ogilvy for Scholastic Inc.

Illustrations: pp. 10-25: Barbara Duke; pp. 26-33: Robert Roper; pp. 54-65: Min Jae Hong; pp. 74-77: Nina Berkson; pp. 112-127: Harvey Chan.